_Ryan._

*Ryan.*

# Rhydderch Jones

yLolfa

Y Lolfa wish to thank Irene Jones and Irene Davies for permission to
reprint the original book; and also to BBC Wales, Y Theatr Newydd,
Raymond Daniel,
*Y Cymro* and *Evening Post* for the pictures.

First published: Black Mountain Press, 1980
New edition: Y Lolfa, 2003
© Irene Jones and Y Lolfa Cyf., 2003

Cover photo: Irene Davies
Cover design: Robat Gruffudd

ISBN: 0 86243 655 9

Published in Wales
and printed on acid-free and partly recycled paper by
Y Lolfa Cyf., Talybont, Ceredigion SY24 5AP
*e-mail* ylolfa@ylolfa.com
*website* ylolfa.com
*phone* (01970) 832 304
*fax* 832 782
*isdn* 832 813

# Preface

IT IS HARD TO BELIEVE that it is twenty five years since Ryan died in April 1977. As a family, our memories of that sad time are as vivid and painful as ever – largely because Ryan is still alive in so many ways. We hear his voice singing on the radio, we hear others performing his compositions, we see him in repeats of *Fo a Fe*, *Ryan a Ronnie* and other programmes that he took part in. The memorial fund continues to finance students who wish to undertake performance-related studies, and of course, there are the anniversary years – 1987, 1997, and of course 2002.

As well as ourselves, his family, there can be no doubt that others who remember Ryan also feel sad when they remember the tragedy that took him from us at the age of forty. It is a testament to Ryan's abilities as a comedian and a performer, and to that incredible charisma, that we can step beyond the sadness, and laugh.

For some years, it was difficult for us children to see Ryan on television and to hear his voice on the radio or on records. Photographs were less difficult to bear, as Mam had kept a few on display at home. With time, of course, it became easier to to watch and listen. In 1996, BBC Cymru scheduled an evening to commemorate the twentieth anniversary of Ryan's death, and I had the opportunity to research and direct one of the programmes: a biography full of archive material, pictures and music. For the first time since his death, I watched every piece of archive film material connected with my father – it was a wonderful experience. As well as laughing and marvelling at the archive programmes, I had the pleasure

*Ryan.*

and privilege of meeting people who had been professionally involved with Ryan, including many who loved him both as a person and a performer. I was phoned by a man who shared digs with Ryan in Shoot Up Hill, London; I talked to a woman from Glais who called her son Ryan; I visited actors like Nerys Hughes and Kenneth Griffith, and caught up with old friends like Margaret Williams, Ronnie, Meredydd Evans, and Glan Davies.

A lot has happened in twenty five years, especially considering that Arwyn and I were children at the beginning of that period. After graduating, I found work with a television company, and I have remained in the industry ever since. I am married and have a little girl, Rebeca Ryan. Arwyn is familiar to many Welsh people as an actor, singer, and composer.

A story like this does not have a happy ending. There is no explanation as to what and who Ryan was. We live our lives just like everyone else, we share the same worries and pleasures as other people. Gladness, sadness, longing and laughter are a difficult combination. If anything positive has come out of this, it is the respect and gratitude towards the audiences, the viewers and the listeners who are still listening, appreciating, remembering, watching and loving, and above all, laughing.

**Bethan Davies**
August 2002

*Ryan with his family: Irene, his wife, Bethan and Arwyn*

I present this book to my god-child Bethan,
Ryan's daughter, and to Irene his wife, and his
son Arwyn.

*Rhydderch Jones*
*16 June, 1980*

# Original Preface

I FIRST MET RYAN with the author on the National Eisteddfod field at Caernarfon in 1959. It was the start of a firm friendship that took Ryan, Rhydderch and myself through many shared experiences during our time in London as amateurs and later in Cardiff.

In all those years, as Ryan's public watched him grow in stature as an entertainer of extraordinary talent, no one was a keener admirer or closer friend than Rhydderch. Every page of this book reflects that closeness as it chronicles Ryan's climb to a pinnacle of success unique, perhaps, in Wales. There can be no doubt that Rhydderch's joy of recalling all those light-hearted incidents, with which this book is packed, was tinged with more than a little pain, but the results of his labours will be read appreciatively by everyone who ever had the pleasure of being entertained by Ryan.

In 1963, I joined the staff of BBC Wales just some few years before the then Head of Light Entertainment, Dr Meredydd Evans, had the vision to offer Ryan a long-term contract for television. The financial security that went with it enabled Ryan to resettle his family in Cardiff and become professional in the full sense of the word. Soon afterwards Rhydderch also joined the BBC and all three of us were, once more, working together – but now getting paid for it!

Ryan quickly mastered the very peculiar techniques required for television through working with many producers, including myself, on a most diverse selection of programmes. But in 1967 came one of the turning points of his career and I mention it only to say how pleased I was to be associated with it. I had been asked to choose a cast and produce a revue-type programme in Welsh. It was an ideal moment to work again with someone whose talent I had admired for so long.

I teamed Ryan with Ronnie Williams, another very able performer and writer, whose father before him had been part of that very successful amateur duo in Wales – Sioni a Iori. Over the next six years, we went on to make some sixty programmes in Welsh and English until such time that the programme titles – 'Ryan a Ronnie' and 'Ryan and Ronnie' became household names throughout the UK.

Those were very challenging but happy years for me.

The rest is documented very fully in this book. It is the biography of a man who was gentle, kind and generous but with a determination to succeed in all that he did. All of us who knew Ryan are pleased that it has been written and no-one could argue that there is anyone better qualified to write it than Rhydderch – his close friend and colleague for so many years. I wish it success.

**David Richards**
Dyffryn, June 1980

# Acknowledgments

IT WAS DIFFICULT FOR ME to write Ryan's biography in Welsh, my own language, since he was a very close friend for twenty years. This version is not a strict translation from my Welsh version; it follows the same course of events for the simple reason that I am writing about the same person. Other people, if they so desire, can be more analytical in their assessment of Ryan as an actor and entertainer; I was much too close to him to be objective. I hope that any young artist, whether singer or actor, by reading this book will learn the most important aspect of this life – it is hard and it needs complete dedication even with the best inherited talent. There are also many aspects of his performances which I have had to explain to non-Welsh speaking people in order that they may fully appreciate them. (I never spoke the English language to Ryan unless there was someone present who couldn't understand Welsh.)

As is evident in this book, I knew Ryan closest in the early years. For a long period I did not work with him and, therefore, I have had to rely upon the help of his friends, fellow artists and press reporters. I would like to take this opportunity to thank the following for all their support:

Owen Edwards (Controller BBC Wales), and Geraint Stanley Jones (Head of Programmes BBC Wales) for kindly allowing me access to scripts, sound and VTR tapes for my reference.

Also, my grateful thanks to:

Mrs. Irene Ryan-Davies, Mrs. Nans Davies (Ryan's mother), Alun Williams, David Richards, Jack Williams, Tom Richards, Marghanita Laski, Bryn Williams, Ronnie Williams, Ifor Lewis, Mari Griffith, Ann Griffiths, Jane Lloyd-Edwards, Edwin Williams, Benny Litchfield, Bryn Richards,

Hywel Gwynfryn, Gwyn Thomas, Iwan Thomas, Ifor Rees, John Hefin, John Chilvers, Richard Lewis, Mervyn Williams and Gillian Thomas.

*Y Cymro, South Wales Evening Post, Y Faner, Liverpool Daily Post, Western Mail, The Times, South Wales Echo, The Observer, Radio Times, Stage & Television Today.*

Jeff Baynham, Brian Watkins, Raymond Daniel, Tegwyn Roberts and Harold Christie.

Selwyn Roderick, Bernard Evans and Jeffrey Iverson for reading, and Betty Evans with Margaret Evans for typing my script.

My wife, Irene, for supporting me during the writing of this book.

I would also like to thank Mike Evans for the great help he has given me in covering Ryan's later years and the dedication he has shown in arranging the publication of this book.

# A Welsh Upbringing

WE ALL BEGIN with a slap on the bum. It's an undignified, even comical ceremony, and no wonder it starts most of us screaming and squeaking on our way into society. When we do, new fathers, new aunties and new uncles dash into warm rooms, open champagne bottles, light cigars. People who have found a new role in life because of our arrival are wrapped in a shawl of merriment and laughter. If these thin screams of ridiculous protest are not heard, everyone retires alone to a cold corner to grieve for what might have been. Tears flow, so that from the first miraculous moment we become a vehicle for pain or happiness.

Playwrights, from the moment they praised Dionysus or tried to win his favour, have written tragedy and comedy back to back – the mask of comedy and the mask of tragedy are always linked together – but hardly ever is there any dialogue between them. To win the Thespian laurel in ancient Greece, the dramatist had to provide three tragedies and one comedy. My friend Ryan spent his life fascinated by the power and the allure of these masks. He wore the mask of comedy for the most part, but always he was strongly aware that the other was trying to utter its lines of dialogue.

Thomas Ryan Davies was born on 22 January, 1937, the son of Nans and William Thomas Davies in the family home, Mountain View, Glanaman on the western edge of the south Wales coalfield. His grandmother on his mother's side, Rachel Roberts, lived there when he was born. Ryan had a favourite joke, the preamble to which went like this:

> My grandmother, my 'mam-gu', had a ranch on the slopes of the Black Mountain, on one of the slopes, that is. Well, it wasn't exactly a ranch, more of a farm, really… you couldn't quite call it

a farm either… not quite. More of a smallholding, if you know
what I mean, with one cow, six chickens and a fat sow.

The 'smallholding' he refers to is the family home where his mother and
her sister Auntie Peggy still live. From many personal experiences, it
epitomizes to me — the kind coal-fire warmth, home-made Welsh cake
taste — what is best in the Aman Valley community, where the human
spirit talks to you without making a din. I met his grandmother, Rachel
Roberts, twice when she was about eighty years old. Looking back over
the year, I vaguely remember a poem by Gwenallt coming to mind after
meeting her for the first time,

> I call to mind my grandmother at Esgeir-ceir
> As she sat, pleating her apron, by the fireside,
> The skin yellow and dry on her face like the manuscript of
>     Peniarth
> And the Welsh on her old lips the Welsh of Pantycelyn.
> A bit of the Puritan Wales, she was of last century.

For better, or for worse, Welsh people have a mania for competition.
We'll compete for chairs, crowns, medals, medallions, batons, before our
intercostals begin to know their function. I hardly know a Welsh person
who has escaped being placed on a chair or table to recite a poem or sing
a song at a ridiculously early age. When Max Boyce, on one of his records,
tells of his experience reciting 'The Squirrel' on a village hall stage with
his mother and a row of aunties mouthing the words in front of him like
goldfish in a bowl, we can all laugh, since we have all been through the
same traumatic experience. This concern with competition may appear
rather simplistic to an outsider, but it has been one of the consuming
passions of our Welsh upbringing. Ryan was brought up in this tradition
at its most virile.

His Uncle Ivor, his mother's brother, was very active with an amateur
operatic company in the Aman Valley. They produced a show every year,

in Welsh and English alternately. Ryan would often tell me this little story about his Uncle Ivor's production of Ivor Novello's 'King's Rhapsody'. Not only did Uncle Ivor produce the show, but he also took the lead. The tickets for this show were very expensive, and the family kept on needling him for those pleasantries which are an anathema to all players and performers – complimentary tickets. Every time the subject was mentioned, Uncle Ivor would blare out in Welsh, 'Can't you understand? Don't you know how much it cost to put this show on the road? A thousand pounds!' And then in English, 'A thousand pounds!' Somehow, that made it sound so much more. He also said the word 'thousand' with an American accent which gave it a further Hollywoodish tinkle. Uncle Ivor, it would appear, had a beautiful voice. Indeed, he won the Blue Ribbon at the Barry National Eisteddfod in 1968. The Blue Ribbon is the accolade of the singing soloists of the festival.

His other uncle on his mother's side, Morgan Rhys Roberts, was famous for his poetry recitation and as an amateur actor. I'll always remember him reciting an ode by Cynan, 'Mab y Bwthyn' ('Son of the Croft'), to Ryan and I from the first word to the last. Cynan was one of our best Welsh lyrical poets, much of whose verse has something of the directness and rhythm of A E Housman's work. Uncle Morgan thundered dramatically through this poem to us on one of the rare and privileged occasions that I met him. A magnificent character, his dramatic career as an amateur actor reached its pinnacle at the Bangor National Eisteddfod in 1931 when he won the main drama prize with a performance of 'Pobl yr Ymylon' ('The Fringe People') by Idwal Jones. This play is a satirical work, where an old tramp is allowed to realise his lifelong ambition – to become a preacher – for one day of his roguish life. It was a great part for Uncle Morgan, and he had gloried in it.

Ryan's father was William Thomas Davies and was the greatest influence on the young lad as he grew up. They were more like two brothers than father and son.

In an article by Pat Searle, angling correspondent to the *Western Mail*, on 27 September, 1975, this is what Ryan has to say concerning his father – it reveals much about both father and son:

> My father, who was the Principal at a home for children, fished in the rivers Cothi and Towy and I learned the delights of chasing the salmon with a Scottish international, a Dr Robert Lindsay. My father left me three rods and a reel, and I hope to put them to good use now that I'm based in an area where fish are as plentiful as early morning rain. My father left me many things; above all, a sense of proportion and love of my country, but his fishing equipment is somehow synonymous with his character. He was a kindly man and he fished the same way. He believed in conservation of life and treated the fish as though they were rare pieces of Dresden china. I, too, am a bit of a conservationist People say I should destroy these little creatures [Ryan refers to a grey squirrel busily nibbling a nut on his lawn during the interview], but to me they're symbols of what I want my children to appreciate – the beauty of the countryside and the lovely living things that surround us.
>
> I worry enormously about the people who condemn our country. They write us off, they make us seem to appear to be living in a dead-end, and when I read and hear about pollution, and the destruction of natural beauty by so-called progress, I wonder where it's all going to end.

These are the words of a mature person, but the seeds of these concepts were planted by Ryan's father when he was a boy:

> In the listening
> Summertime of the dead whispered the truth of his joy
> To the trees and the stones and the fish in the tide.

Because of his parents' work as wardens of local government hostels, Ryan spent a somewhat nomadic youth, but all of it in west Wales. The family lived in Nantgaredig, Llangadog, Llandovery, Felinfoel, and Llanfyllin in Montgomeryshire. At Nantgaredig, his parents ran a children's home. For some unknown reason it burned to the ground – nobody was hurt, thank heavens – and Ryan once said, "It had nothing to do with me!"

Although he spent his boyhood in all these places for varying periods, Glanaman remained nearest to his affections. His roots were firmly set in the sour soil of the Black Mountain. This was the 'square mile' to which he returned as often as his busy life allowed. When Ryan was ten, his parents moved to Llanfyllin in Powys to take charge of an old people's home called Y Dolydd.

When he first saw the Dolydd, Ryan was struck with the sombre bleakness of the stone building, especially the part called 'the casual ward'. This part was reserved for the occasional tramp to put down his head to rest for the night. He remembered one old hobo in particular, named Bobbie Burns. This one-eyed hero was very clever with his hands and made little ships out of silver paper for the wide-eyed admirer. It is not beyond contention to think that living under the same roof as the elderly inhabitants of the Dolydd gave Ryan an early mature understanding of character. They certainly provided him with an audience; Ryan and his father used to perform for the pleasure of those old folks.

Ryan's father became the organist at Moriah chapel, and accompanist to the Llanfyllin mixed choir, which he also later conducted. As Ryan himself records, "When I first came to Llanfyllin, we had three choirs – mixed, male and a children's choir. Whereas my father was involved with both the mixed and the male, I sang with the children's choir."

His teacher in the primary school was the late Mr Ifor Lewis. This kind gentleman was a native of my own little village, Aberllefenni, and it was Mr Ifor Lewis who nurtured the young lad as a singer. Before his death, Mr Lewis told me the story:

> When Ryan was ten years old, the Powys Eisteddfod was held in Llanfyllin. Ryan was reciting under twelve and also under

fifteen. He was also singing under twelve and under fifteen, and singing with the harp under fifteen. Prizes fell upon him like confetti. The compere was a man called Llwyd o'r Bryn, still a legend amongst the eisteddfodic legions, often caricatured orally because of his pronunciation of the consonant 'r', which he rolled with guttural exuberance. Seeing Ryan coming up for prizes time and time again he said, "This lad Brian is on the stage oftener than I am".

It was the first time he sang with the harp, but he won first prize anyway. Singing poetry to the accompaniment of the harp (penillion singing) is an art peculiar to the Welsh people. In this competition he was accompanied by veteran artiste Nansi Richards, a highly-accomplished Welsh triple harpist. This harp, again peculiar to the Welsh, has three rows of strings, where semitones are attained by fingering the middle row. Even to the uninitiated, it is rather obvious that this art demands enormous dexterity of the digits. Nansi Richards later gave Ryan a few preliminary lessons, but although he learned to play the ordinary harp, he never mastered the triple harp.

When Ryan moved on to secondary school, he was again fortunate to have a very good headmaster. Ryan came to admire Mr J Lloyd Thomas greatly; indeed, he talked of him with deep affection and admiration. He was an integral influence in moulding the character of a young boy who was to become our country's greatest entertainer. Ryan particularly remembered one occasion during his school career and he often spoke proudly of it. To commemorate the opening of a new extension to the school, it was decided to produce a concert of Haydn's 'The Seasons'. Ryan was asked to sing the tenor part and the soprano part was sung by the now internationally-famous opera singer Elizabeth Vaughan. They sang together many times after that.

Mr W J Jones, his Welsh master at Llanfyllin, remembers that during the drama competition at the school, both his own department and the English one fought tooth and nail for the young thespian's services. The first time he stepped on to the boards was in a little play involving a ride on a wooden horse, for which he composed a song. The other play was a translation of 'Money for Nothing' by Morton Haward, when he apparently gave a vivid performance.

Amongst the galaxy of memories the Welsh master had of endless pupils, one recollection of Ryan outshone all others: "I remember him playing the piano in the morning assembly. Somehow, when he played, he was able to bring out a feeling that was not there at other times". It was the first suggestion of a strange gift of Ryan's that is only given to a few mortals – the ability to project one's emotions to many in that one moment of time.

Ryan was no fool on the playing field, either, and it is curious to know that the little urchin, thin as a biro refill, was almost as dexterous with a ball as he was with a piano. During these young years he was selected to play cricket for the county of Montgomery. He recalled, "I was considered to be a bit of a batsman, and I was also quite agile at catching a ball". He even played soccer for Llanfyllin, as a goalkeeper. I suppose that if you can catch a small hard ball, catching a bigger soft one is easy meat!

In the more mundane aspects of school life, such as learning, he was not so keen. Interviewed in front of a classroom of children much later in life, Ryan commented upon his academic prowess: "I didn't like examinations. They had a strange effect on me. I worried too much about them and they affected my health. Of course, had I known the work better, this might not have occurred".

His best friend at school was a boy named Brian Jones, who now lives in Buffalo, New York State, and who remained his close friend for the rest of his life. It was at this time that he also met the best of his best friends, a young girl named Irene Williams. Irene came from Llanrhaeadr-ym-Mochnant; they were both fourteen years old at the time. In an interview with the *South Wales Evening Post* in March 1978, these were Irene's words: "Even in his schooldays, Ryan had a charming personality.

19

He had a genuine love of people, and people came close to him. There was an enormous warmth in his character, and this attracted an audience to him."

It is difficult to put together the jigsaw of the myriad facets that make up the pattern of a boy growing up, but it would appear that Ryan became a young man who had a love of nature, a talent for projecting human emotions in music and words, a love of family, and a fear of failure. Ryan also had a real fear of God, of which more later. All these are human traits, probably more pronounced in the make-up of the Celtic peoples, because of our star-crossed history and the nature of our parental upbringing.

Leaving school, Britain said she needed Ryan, and he ended up serving his national service with the Brylcreem brigade, the Royal Air Force. After ten weeks of strenuous, bone-shaking torture called 'square-bashing', he landed in what he once described to me as 'a hush-hush hole' in England. The romantic heroism of the boys in blue had long dwindled to obscurity, and plotting the comings and goings of harmless jets was as boring as lying on a barrack-room bed watching the flight of equally harmless houseflies. However, the lowest-ranked airman in Britain, it would appear, became more successful than the Air Chief Marshal when, on payday nights, he played the piano in the 'Naafi'.

The best thing the Royal Air Force ever did for Ryan was to permit him to return his blue uniform, webbing, and blanco three weeks before his national service expired, so that he could enter the strangely-named Normal College at Bangor, north Wales.

# In the Normal

ANYONE WHO HAS SERVED with the armed forces, and who has had the dubious privilege of slamming his hob-nailed boots into unyielding concrete, believes that everyone from lance-corporal upwards is essentially a sadist. Thus it came to pass that many of those young men who had practised a 'two-fingered' exercise on military authority a few minutes *after* their demob found themselves in a similar predicament to Ryan. The Normal College, Bangor, north Wales, had been founded one hundred years, minus one, to the year 1958. It was apparently established for the sole purpose of teaching people to teach. Some who arrived there in 1958 had survived tougher military marathons than Ryan in his 'hush-hush hole somewhere in England'. A few had hacked their way through the semi-tropical jungles of Malaya, à là 'the virgin soldiers'. A few had seen comrades bleed to death, and one or two knew how to kill a human being with their own – or even the victim's – shoe-lace.

When we arrived at the Normal College, it was one hell of a surprise for us all to find that we had to assemble at the Common Room every evening at ten thirty, half an hour after the pubs closed. We were embarrassed to discover that university students, who had just been unleashed from their mother's apron strings, were allowed to gambol freely until unearthly hours without any constraint, while we had to 'clock-in' every night. Small wonder that a boxing match, arranged at a later time between the University and the Normal, became a vehicle for frustration. The eight-bout match lasted only half an hour; the longest contest was forty-five seconds. Conceit and arrogance brought the Normal victory by eight bouts to nil.

*Ryan.*

The college principal was Dr Richard Thomas. One student became renowned amongst his budding Pestalozzis for his unique Welsh ability of speaking everyday, domestic utterances in 'cynghanedd'. 'Cynghanedd' is an ancient Welsh poetic art which has something to do with assonance, alliteration and onomatopoeia. Even if you are fortunate enough to appreciate such classic lines of English verse as:

> The moan of doves in immemorialelms
> And murmuring of innumerable bees,

You still haven't a clue about 'cynghanedd'. Yet this fellow student could speak in the rhythms of this complex verse. He was a wonder, and referred to our principal with his alliterative nickname, 'Dic Tom the Dictator'. This gentleman ruled his college with a rod of iron. Indeed, within a few weeks of enrolling, Ryan was summoned to his office and threatened with dismissal for committing the revolutionary act of smoking on the stairs between lectures.

The men's hostel – the George – nestled on the banks of the Menai Straits. Looking out of our dormitory windows, four hundred yards to the left one could see a majestic suspension bridge, the gateway to Anglesey. One mile, five hundred yards, and six inches to the right, beyond our view, nestled the nearest women's hostel! We nicknamed the George 'Stalagluft'.

One of three things inevitably happens to a crowd of young men barbwired for a second time in their lives. They either throw bombs, carry placards denouncing the system, or they defeat the system by guile. If one knows how to get out of a military encampment, getting out of a college hostel is like shooting rats in a barrel. Even the George could never compete with Colchester Barracks. One room, inevitably belonging to the students' entertainment secretary, had an exit leading to the fire escape. The poor man reached the end of term counting male students in his sleep rather than women. Few exited down the iron steps, but many more entered that way than through the official portals. By the end of the first term, the poor entertainment secretary was a complete neurotic!

At the witching hour of half past ten, we were herded into the Common Room. The duty lecturer called our names, from Bates to Yeates, and vanished. After the fire escape freeway was put to full use, it was hard to contain one's amusement when a name was called out, and answered by an imitated voice. Later in the day, Ryan became an expert at this game, and could mimic 'Here, sir' in different voices, while the real owners of the voices were up to no good on the merry, mossy banks of Menai Woods.

However, having got over the initial shock of the disciplinary atmosphere, the college became very dear to all of us and 'Stalagluft' became a home, a chocolate castle nestling in an idyllic spot by the dangerous, beautiful Straits.

We inherited a particular tradition from our forerunners. After the president of the students' union had completed the serious business of student life, such as announcing the rugby and soccer scores, humorous business took over. At this juncture one student would stand up and accuse another, usually his best friend, of causing a misdemeanour that was injurious to the good name of the hostel and the chivalry of his colleagues. One student took the 'humorous business' so seriously that he waddled around the common room like Charles Laughton in the film 'Witness for the Prosecution'. The accused then had a chance to defend himself, and the matter was put to the vote. The losing party was then expected to 'recite, sing, or do the other thing', the 'other thing' being an attempted dash from the sanctuary of the common room. If his attempt failed he was thrown into a bath of cold water. I regularly accused Ryan, the dialogue being something along these lines:

"Mr Chairman."

"Mr Jones."

"This morning, at approximately ten thirty, in an English Literature lecture on 'Paradise Lost', Mr Ryan Davies said that the divine, sacred poet John Milton was, in his opinion, a sex maniac [Derisive shouts of

'Disgusting', 'Shame']. Mr Chairman, I do not believe that Mr Ryan Davies made this statement with the intention of advancing the cause of English literature, but for a personal, calculated, underhanded reason. First of all, I believe that he wanted to see if the lady lecturer would blush [Shouts]; secondly, he wanted to find how many of the women students would blush; lastly, he wanted to know how many of the women students wouldn't blush [Shouts]. I hope, Mr Chairman, that Mr Ryan Davies will be found guilty on all three charges."

Ryan would get up to defend himself but inevitably, whether he was the accused or the accuser, he would be found guilty, since everyone in the common room wanted to hear and see him perform. It was on the round table in the middle of the students' common room, in circumstances similar to those I have just quoted, that I heard Ryan perform for the first time. The act was that of whistling 'In a Monastery Garden' à là Ronnie Ronalde.

The only student Ryan could get 'on the table' was a good friend of ours, Wil Williams, now a teacher in Ruthin. It was discovered early in the term that Wil was tone deaf, and would sing 'If You Were the Only Girl in the World' from beginning to end on one, single, solitary, high note.

In those days, apart from the essential subjects of Education, Child Psychology, and Health and Hygiene, each student could choose a main subject and three subsidiary subjects, one of which had to be a scientific one. Ryan chose English Literature as his main study, and Music, Dramatic Art, and General Science as his subsidiaries. In actual fact he only ever attended one lecture in General Science. This subject seemed to be very popular with aspiring students. At the first attendance, the laboratory was full of budding Newtons. Every chair was occupied, and many students were sitting on the workbenches dangling their feet, with their bums near bunsen burners. The lecturer must have felt dejected at the idea of facing such a multitude for two long years. He decided to give a lecture on Einstein's theory of relativity. He covered the blackboard with intricate formulas and calculus that ended with the well-known formula $E=MC^2$. How he arrived at such a conclusion was a mystery to all present. However, most, indeed all the students present believed that only Einstein himself could have understood such mathematical logic. Most of the budding Newtons – including Ryan – having faced such an avalanche of knowledge, decided not to attend another lecture. He embarked upon a more homely subject, Rural Science, which he personally nicknamed 'diggin', without the 'g'. Scholastic life became much more relaxing when the only scientific knowledge required was that sufficient to perform the rustic act of growing spuds, rather than that required to split the atom!

In my experience, the familiar notion that opposites attract is hardly ever true in terms of human beings. In barracks, classrooms, or lecture halls, people of similar natures, whims and aspirations soon team together. In the Normal College, there were students who hardly breathed fresh air, being continually engrossed in theories of education and their chosen subjects. Some occasionally dared to visit a cafe in Upper Bangor for a cup of tea and a blushing wink at a female student. But they would never take her to the back seat of the Plaza Cinema. Then there was another crowd that shared their textbooks, and left a very large slice of their grant in the till of the Antelope, the pub by the Menai suspension bridge. John Huw Evans (Huwcyn) from Borth, near Aberystwyth – now an assistant headmaster in Croydon; Dan Roberts from Arthog near Dolgellau – now a representative of the NUT; Wil Williams, whom I've already mentioned; John Richard Jones – now a school advisory officer in the Swansea Valley, Ryan, and myself could all be found only too often propping up the bar in the Antelope. We all developed a slight addiction to pies and pints.

Two students, who had shared their National Service jumping out of aeroplanes with the Parachute Regiment, decided to buy a motorbike. They were particularly attracted to this two-wheeled monster, and they roared to and fro from the town to the hostel as if they were in the Isle of Man. They tested providence once too often, and were challenged one evening by a member of the constabulary. It was discovered that neither had a driving licence, road fund licence, or insurance. As they were new students, who had only just finished serving Queen and Country, the constable was very lenient with them. He told them to come to the police station the following morning. They did so – to face a lecture on law and order – riding the motorbike!

That was the most anti-social act that I remember any of us performing, but every other day amongst ourselves, someone or other tried to pull someone's leg. It was one-upmanship in tomfoolery. Once a term, a fire drill was held by Mr 'Bell' Davies, a mathematics lecturer who was also fire officer for the George. As soon as the fire bell rang through the corridors, he would start his stopwatch. It was an age-old tradition that every year should try to beat their predecessors' record. Carrying one item only – the most prized of all our worldly possessions – we would dash like bats out of hell into the yard. One cock-eyed optimist, suffering from myopia and a lack of agility, carried a picture of a semi-naked Marilyn Monroe. The stopwatch stopped, and we would stand in the yard like the heroes in the film 'The Bridge over the River Kwai', while Mr Davies counted us. Depending on the state of our attire at the moment the bell rang, it was an incongruous sight – some would be in vest and underpants or a solitary towel, others in football gear, another who had served in Malaya would sport a kimono, while a few idiots would be on unnecessary crutches. One term, Mr Davies congratulated us for breaking the college record. The shout of jubilation was broken by another shout from the top of the fire escape. It was Huwcyn and Wil, dressed as two nurses, carrying Ryan in rugby togs strapped to a stretcher singing at the top of his voice some ridiculous song such as 'Take Me to the Garden, Maud'. Although our Olympic record had gone out of the window, we created a new record for laughter.

During the second term of our first year, Ryan and I began writing songs; Ryan composing the music, and I the words. Together with Wil Ifor Jones and Phil Hughes, Ryan formed the Normal College Trio. Sometimes Geraint Jones, now Head of Presentation with BBC Wales, would take over. The songs we wrote in those days were very old-fashioned compared to the popular songs of today. We established a college party which toured the Bangor area performing a 'Noson Lawen', which translates literally as 'a Merry Night'. The idea is similar to the Irish and Scottish ceilidh or to the Breton 'Fest Noz'. Its origins lie in rural areas where people gather on the hearth or in the barn for homespun entertainment. Ryan and I performed at hundreds of such evenings in the years to come, but the first-ever stands out in my mind. It was at Cwm-y-Glo in Arfon, in the village hall, lit by stable lamps. I was compering the evening and, for some reason or other, I recited a simple line of 'cynghanedd' in Welsh, 'Môr o jam yw Meri Jane' – 'Mary Jane is a sea of jam'. Even if you understood Welsh and appreciated the fun of alliteration, it is not a particularly funny line, but the audience broke into undulating fits of laughter. This was a mystery to Ryan and myself until we discovered that a local character, well-endowed with layers of adipose connective tissue, was sitting a few rows from the stage, and her name was Mary Jane! Upon hearing her own name, and hearing the audience laughing, she herself started laughing, and wobbled like a blancmange. Laughter in some circumstances can become contagious, and sometimes uncontrollable. Poor Mary Jane had to be taken out of the hall! I am quite convinced that it was during these evenings that Ryan started getting to know his audience.

As well as his whistling act, playing the piano, and singing, Ryan started to develop the art of mime. This delicate art of making silence talk is very difficult, but it is one of the actor's most effective weapons. Whereas the ancient actors of Greece and Rome sometimes used this art to propagate political propaganda, Ryan tried, like other artists before him, to use this gift to convey humour. He'd walk cockily into á café, sit by a table, and he'd confidently call a waiter. He'd order a menu and wave to a person at another table. The person would appear to recognise him. He'd turn his head only to find that the person whom he'd thought he recognised was only acknowledging someone at another table, then he'd register complete embarrassment. The soup would arrive. He'd look into the bowl only to discover that it was inhabited by an eel-shaped monster that one could just see with the wriggling movement of Ryan's head… it was really there, and it was really alive! The monster would jump out of the soup bowl… Ryan would take a few steps, and with a stamp of his foot, the 'thing' would be expunged. The village halls of Snowdonia had seen nothing like it since the silent films of Chaplin – and neither had I. Then the second course – a solitary small fish with six chips – would arrive, and Ryan would complain to the people at the opposite table, whom he didn't know. From Ryan's expressions, it was obvious that they were not interested, and were embarrassed by his complaints. The dessert would be custard and the inevitable prunes. He would 'spit' the stones at the people at the next table for their lack of support. The waiter would return with an astronomical bill. Ryan would get to his feet with an upward tilt of his eye. The waiter was obiously a Titan. With exaggerated servility, he would pay the bill, and leave the restaurant. This mime that Ryan performed without a single utterance gave pleasure to hundreds if not thousands of people during the years that were to come. I saw him perform it countless times, yet there was something fresh, some added facet, in every performance.

The Welsh are not renowned for their humour, possibly because we haven't had much to laugh about. Many say the religious revivals and Bible-thumping preachers have knocked the hell out of us, and that we have developed a syndrome that does not allow us even to titter, especially at ourselves. The humour that we do possess is either a very dry one, or the complete opposite – blundering jokes. I believe that Ryan was the first Welsh actor to convey the subtle Welsh humour; indeed, the pathos of our humour. Call it the tear in the clown's eye, if you will. I mention this aspect of his performance at such an early stage because one felt, even in the mime I have just mentioned, that the audience were not simply laughing at the funny actions, but that they somehow empathised with the little man.

It was around this time that Ryan and myself made contact with the BBC. A female student and myself were asked to take part in the Inter-college Debate in Bangor. A few hours before the event, I was trembling with fear. I had arranged to meet Ryan in an Upper Bangor pub, so that I could rehearse the oration with him. The subject was, "It is a disgusting thing to put a woman in a sack". My speech dealt with the motion from a male chauvinistic assertion that all women should be put down – cast into a river like drowning kittens! Ryan told me, "It's not that kind of sack, idiot, it's the sack dress, it's not a sack – sack".

Ryan was always with it and up on the latest fashion trends, whereas to me, 'vogue' was just a word in a dictionary. However, we changed my speech and, indeed, the female student and I won the competition.

The instigator of this series, like many other popular series in the Welsh language was the late Sam Jones, later to be honoured by the University of Wales with a Doctorate in Literature for his contribution to radio programmes. He was a small, wiry man, full of enthusiasm. He asked Ryan and myself to meet him in his office at the BBC. He told us of a radio programme he produced when he was a young man. It was a religious programme he had recorded in the bowels of a coal mine, and the miners had held a midday service. I believe he told us it was his first programme ever. However, he introduced us to Adam's Ifor Rees, now a producer with BBC Wales; and we gave our first-ever radio performance on Ifor's Welsh programme, 'Asbri'. Ifor tells me that Ryan once appeared on one of his programmes as a young lad, but there is no record of this. For this first broadcast, we were paid ten shillings and sixpence each – half a guinea in the old money – Ryan for the music, myself for the words. I am sorry to say (or am I?) that we left every last penny in the till of the Antelope.

Throughout our formative years, our destinies are influenced by the abilities – or lack thereof – of our teachers and lecturers. Ryan's career was strongly influenced by Adam's Edwin Williams, the first drama lecturer at the Normal College. This was the first time drama had been taught at the college, and we were incredibly lucky that this new venture coincided with our entry to the college. Ryan was studying Drama through the medium of English under Edwin, and he was taught the history of drama from Aristophanes to Shaw. He was also learning how to plot stage movement, makeup, and the many disciplines that make up the actor's art. He learnt how to project his voice, the dramatic use of pause, and how to control his speech. In retrospect, I believe that Ryan inherently possessed many of these qualities – he was an actor by instinct – but Edwin was the first person to harness these attributes. Ryan's greatest quality was his uncanny sensitivity to sound. He was the person with the most sensitive ear I have ever known.

In 1957 the city of Bangor was endowed with three cinemas – the posh Plaza and two fleapits. These cinemas showed two films per week and their greatest attribute was their showing of matinees. Ryan and I were supposed to attend lectures in what were referred to as subsidiary subjects – History and Geography. I am embarrassed that my knowledge of geography is so incredibly parochial even in this jet-setting age. Until a few years ago, I thought that Monte Carlo was in America. When Ryan and I wrote our second song, a romantic song about Paris dedicated to Irene, his girlfriend, I asked him, "Ry, can you hear the bells of Notre Dame from the River Seine?"

"What do you mean, 'from the Seine', you bloody fool?" he replied. "Notre Dame is on the Seine!"

Despite our lack of historical and geographical knowledge, we knew and discussed every film that appeared in the cinemas of Bangor for two years; we even fantasised about presenting Oscars to each one, according to our own evaluation of what we had seen. When the History and Geography lecturers complained about our absence, Edwin would always stick up for us, saying that we were in drama rehearsals.

Returning to the concept of Ryan's sensitive hearing; on one particularly wet afternoon, we visited a fleapit showing 'Our Girl Friday'. We expected it to be a sensual, sexy drama about a young man and woman cast together on an island and having to learn about the birds and the bees from scratch. The film was true to the anticipated theme, but Ryan and I found it incredibly boring and the young actress, despite her curvaceous topography, appeared to us to be as flat as a plank. Disappointed with our Girl Friday, we decided to leave the cinema. Suddenly, however, the 'B' feature appeared; a film called 'The Glass Mountain'. We sat in seats further along the row, and Ryan became mesmerized by this film, a melodrama about an orchestral conductor. Afterwards, Ryan and I walked up what was then called Jimmy's Hill to the Kit Rose cafe; he spoke not a word to me all the way, but he sat at the piano in this cafe and repeatedly played the theme song from the film. To my knowledge he had never heard it before, but I believe he played it exactly as it had been played in the cinema.

I remember something else about Ryan's sensitive hearing. Every student in the college had to take a course in phonetics. Had I not come across Professor Pickering in Shaw's 'Pygmalion' I would have remained unaware of the existence of such a system of symbols. To me, all the letters looked like hieroglyphics, but Ryan was in his element from the first lecture and by the end of the course, he could write phonetics freely.

In those days, it was a tradition in the Normal College for the Welsh and English Societies to take turns to produce a play in alternate terms. During our first term it was the Welsh Society's turn, and Edwin decided to produce a translation by Saunders Lewis of Molière's 'Le Médecin Malgré Lui'. I was chosen to play the lead – the part of Sganarelle, the wood cutter – because of the roguish nature of the character, I suppose! Ryan played the part of Valère, the nobleman Geroti's main servant. The stylized acting associated with Molière's comedy was up his street. He received his first notice as an actor in the Welsh newspaper, *Y Faner*, in December 1957. "We had excellent acting from Ryan Davies (Valère) and Philip Hughes (Lucas) in their masterly portrayal of the social conventions of the eighteenth century."

His movements and gestures were incredibly funny, and he was much happier onstage than he was in a lecture room. Edwin was a first-class stage producer, and he had a great influence on the young actor's development.

1958 was the centenary of the Normal College, and it was celebrated with bun fights, concerts, exhibitions, and open days and Edwin decided to put on a special performance under the auspices of the English Society. He chose a play by Christopher Fry called 'The Lady is not for Burning'. This springtime comedy was first produced at a club theatre, and later successfully staged on Shaftesbury Avenue in 1949 by Sir John Gielgud, a success which was repeated on Broadway. Ryan was chosen to play the lead, a character called Thomas Mendip, played by the great Welsh actor Richard Burton in the original production. The verse-play was greatly in vogue around 1950, when journalists predicted a revival of poetic drama. However, the prediction was short-lived and after John Osborne's play 'Look Back in Anger' was produced in 1956, the 'kitchen sink' drama took over. The comedy 'The Lady is not for Burning' shows Fry's brilliant verbal gift, and is a celebration of life, but the poetry does not always advance or clarify the action. The syntax of his sentences is incredibly complex; a great challenge to any young actor. However, Ryan and Mary Rees, a fellow student, gave brilliant performances. His tongue slipped gently and harshly through the crags and craters of Fry's lines; lines such as the following, which Ryan quoted to me many times after this performance: 'The moon is nothing but a circumambulatory aphrodisiac, divinely subsidized to provoke the world into a rising birthrate'. It is one hell of a complicated way of saying 'Give me the moonlight, give me the girl'!

Ryan was highly praised for his portrayal of Thomas Mendip and, when I look back at those days, I do not believe that I am far wrong in saying that it was this performance that gave him the sniff of the greasepaint. I believe that Ryan had found his niche – the stage would support him in the future. The aforementioned Cynan was then Archdruid of Wales; he was in the audience during a performance of 'The Lady is not for Burning'.

He was so impressed by the production that he invited Edwin Williams to put on a production at the National Eisteddfod held in Caernarfon in 1959. However, there were more mundane drudgeries, such as lectures and exams, to attend to in the meantime.

*Ryan.*

*Ryan at an early age
on the lawns of his
grandmother's ranch...*

*...and posing with his
own stock of one cow,
six chickens and a fat sow.*

*September 1955 – outside the N.A.A.F.I. while serving Queen and Country. "In a hole somewhere in England."*

*Ryan, Ieuan Davies and the author in a sketch about baby food.*

*Ryan as Thomas Mendip with Mary Rees in Christopher Fry's 'The Lady's Not For Burning'. It was this performance which formed the basis for his future theatrical career.*

_Ryan._

Margaret Lewis, Mari Vaughan-Jones, Ryan and the author in the play 'A Oes Heddwch?', a translation of 'The Offshore Island' by Marghanita Laski, at the Rhos National Eisteddfod, 1961.

Ryan, the author, Ieuan Davies and Hafina Clwyd in a sketch with the London Welsh Society branch of the Urdd, circa 1960.

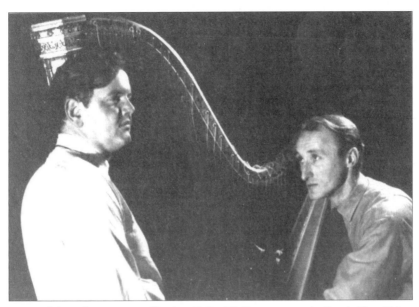

*Ryan and the author singing penillion in a St David's Day concert at the Royal Albert Hall.*

*As Fancourt Babberley in 'Charley's Aunt' at the Llanelli National Eisteddfod.*

*Ryan.*

*In a folk-dancing group at a garden party in London. Howard, Janice, Huwcyn, Janet, and Irene with Ryan.*

*Dennis Griffiths with Alun Davies, Ryan and Bryn Richards – The Three Taffs – making a television programme circa 1963.*

*St John's School Choir on a visit to the Llangollen International Eisteddfod.*

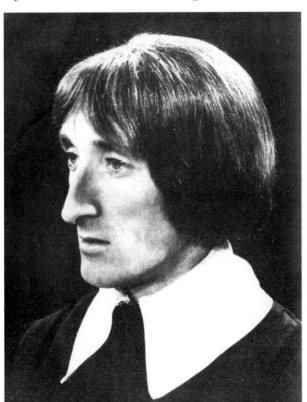

*Acting the part of Morgan Llwyd at Llandudno National Eisteddfod.*

39

*Ryan.*

*With Charles Williams in the programme 'O Lan i Lan' ('From Village to Village').*

*The little man with the bowler hat.*

*Touching up the ivories.*

_Ryan._

_"There are moments when a clown can be serious."_

*A variety of roles in which Ryan appeared in late 1966. The series was called 'Igam Ogam' and Ryan set out to prove himself an expert in various fields – but something always seemed to go wrong!*

*Ryan.*

*Dickensian Ryan.*

*"Forget about the funny bits —
what about Palestrina?"*

*Performing in a series produced by Ieuan Davies for Teledu Cymru, with Emyr Edwards.*

'Pros Kairon', his first appearance with the Welsh Theatre Company as a professional actor.

*Ryan.*

*Ryan and Ronnie outside the
BBC Television Theatre,
Shepherds Bush, before recording
their first English series.*

*Ryan and Ronnie seal their
partnership with a three-year
contract for the BBC.*

*A sketch at Portmeirion for the Ryan and Ronnie television series.*

*In a Ryan and Ronnie film,
he tries to cross 'The Little Border'.*

# A Pigeon and a Farewell to Bangor

EVER SINCE I WAS A YOUNG LAD, I had worked on a farm with my friend Dafydd Jones during college holidays. On one occasion, it was too wet to harvest the hay, so I was sent with a big scythe to cut bracken on the mountainous slope above the little village of Corris. I can think of no worse torture, other than the punishment of lying on the burning lake of hell, as meted out to the fallen angels in Milton's 'Paradise Lost'. My sinews were aching, and I was contemplating the idiocy of Kronos cutting slices of the sky, Uranus, with a scythe, hoping that one of them would come down from Olympus or Cader Idris to relieve me, when I suddenly heard a shout from earth – the bottom of the valley. A car had stopped on the old road from Corris to its sister village of Upper Corris. A small figure was climbing the fence and coming up towards me, waving frantically. When he came near enough I recognised him – it was Ryan. Over acres of bracken he shouted at me,

"I'm engaged!"

"To who?"

"Irene, of course!"

The gods had granted my wish. This was delightful news; Mercury himself never brought better tidings. I threw the scythe, an implement that I wasn't particularly fond of by this time, into a nearby hedge and went with Ryan to celebrate.

Irene had been Ryan's girlfriend since their school days, but during the last term at college, he'd met another girl. I believe she had helped with the stage make-up in 'The Lady is not for Burning', but that particular lady didn't simmer long either! When Ryan had returned from college at the end of term, his parents had sensed that all was not well at Camelot!

Irene was teaching in England by this time, and was returning home. They asked him to pick her up at the station in Oswestry. During our little celebration on the wet day he told me the story:

"She stepped off the train, I proposed to her, and she accepted before the train left the station".

I think he was showing off a little when he made that statement. Irene told me later that it was only after driving for miles in silence that he plucked up enough courage to propose to her. Reading too much Byron must have given him a sense of romantic grandeur! Irene had been born and bred in the village of Llanrhaeadr-ym-Mochnant not far from Llanfyllin. Like Ryan, she was steeped in the traditions of our music, folk-dancing and the eisteddfod. She was very different to Ryan in temperament and she was a very steadying influence on him. Ryan could have long depressive moods, and then, like a barometer in a thunderstorm, he'd suddenly be on cloud nine.

I visited the Dolydd regularly in those days. I remember an old lady, Annie, a resident at the old people's home who helped Ryan's mother around the house. She pampered Ryan like a broody old hen and spoilt him with her affection, and her affection was returned; Ryan thought the world of her. Sunday dinners at the Dolydd were a feast, and Ryan's father was an expert at making mushy peas. One afternoon Ryan, Irene, a girlfriend of hers and I went a-courting – Ryan driving. I couldn't drive a wheelbarrow, let alone a car. Besides that, I didn't own a car – or a wheelbarrow for that matter. We 'accidentally on purpose' found ourselves in one of Powys' remote leafy glades. Ryan and Irene went to the back seat of the car, and I had to sit in the driver's seat with the 'friend' in the passenger seat. As I tried unsuccessfully to make rather innocent romantic advances, I saw some travellers approaching. I warned Ryan of the advancing intrusion, and when the busybodies stared through the steaming car window I peeped over my shoulder, only to find that both Ryan and Irene had vanished under a handy travelling rug. When I returned to my home village I sent him a poem in Welsh, in 'cynghanedd'. It is impossible to translate such a poem, but the last line read, 'Mating under material'.

The Welsh will write poetry at the drop of an adjective! It is a rural custom to send a poem if someone gets married, dies, or is 'caught with his pants down' – and I don't mean that literally. To return to the business of 'cynghanedd'; whereas most poets take this art very seriously, others use it as a vehicle of fun. A few English poets have tried to use this complicated form of assonance in their serious work, most notably Gerard Manley Hopkins in such poems as 'The Wreck of the Deutschland'. Some poets have come up with fun-poems in English. An elegy to a bookmaker, for example, ends

> But aft*er* a *bitter/bet*
> **er b – er b**
> *The* bookie/kicked *the* b*ucket*
> **Th –b – k-      th –b – k•**

Each line consists of seven syllables, with the monosyllabic word 'bet' rhyming more or less with the bisyllabic word 'bucket'. In the first line there is an internal rhyme between 'after' and 'bitter', and the 'b' in 'bitter' alliterates with the 'b' in 'bet'. In the second line, the consonants 'th', 'b' and 'k' are repeated in the second half of the line. However, although neither Ryan nor I hardly ever wrote a correct line, we had a lot of fun with our funny attempts at writing in this metre. The chair, the accolade of the Welsh poet, is awarded for a poem involving this kind of metre. Ryan and I would be unlikely to win a commode with our efforts!

The Colditz-like atmosphere of the Normal College vanished after we returned to our second year in 1958. The previous principal, who had ruled with a rod of iron, had retired. His position had been taken by Adam's Edward Rees, a kind, understanding man, and very soon the students developed a deep affection for him. He treated us as mature people, invited us to his home and took an interest in our social functions as well as our academic ones.

Our entertainment troupe flourished, and we were gaining popularity in North Wales, travelling from hamlet to hamlet like a troop of minstrels. Although only about twelve of us took an active part, often two bus-loads of students would converge on an innocent village. We had more supporters, or hangers-on, than the college rugby team or even the women's hockey team, and that really was popularity! Sometimes there would be more students in the audience than local people. Once, we ventured over the border to England, if Liverpool can be called a part of England. That evening, I could have sworn that the great city was just an extension of North Wales. Dafydd Morgan, a reporter with the Welsh paper *Y Cymro* (The Welshman), reported thus:

> *[Translation]* The party of talented young people that came from the banks of the Menai to the banks of the Mersey was like a breath of fresh air from Wales to the two hundred and fifty Welsh people that assembled in Waterloo Chapel hall, Liverpool, to spend an entertaining evening. The party from the Normal College, Bangor, gave two and a half hours of Welsh light entertainment, and what an enthusiastic welcome they received from the keen Liverpool Welsh. The hall was packed, and more chairs had to be brought in before the entertainment commenced. I have never seen such an appreciative audience.

He writes of Ryan in his report: "Ryan Davies from Llanfyllin (singing, miming, playing the piano) – a young man of great versatile talent".

These shows, these audiences, these unadorned stages were certainly the stamping grounds where Ryan developed his art of comedy. It is also only fair to say that these audiences, which gave him the opportunity, received his adulation for the rest of his life. He had started to develop another mime by this time. He had tried it out 'on the table' using his fellow-students as guinea pigs before, but now he started performing it in public. It was a mime about a driving lesson. Ryan was the driver and the absent instructor seemed to be confused as he tried to understand the indicators, even before the car had started. He gave an impression, through his miming, that the car was in such an archaic condition that you wouldn't even enter it in an old crocks race, let alone venture onto a public highway with it. The gearstick detached itself from the rest of his charabanc during the hilarious ride that ended with the inevitable crash. In these shows, he was a wizard on the piano, although I don't think he could read music particularly well in those days. He played mostly by ear, but he could do almost anything with an old 'joanna', other than make it dance. He would accompany his audience in a well-known song and then, just as they were getting into the spirit of the song, he'd go up a semitone, then another semitone, putting his bewildered audience out of tune!

We continued to write songs together for the trio, who appeared quite often on the radio programme 'Asbri', produced by Ifor Rees.

One other 'Noson Lawen' remains in my memory. We had a booking – the fee was the cost of two coaches from Bangor to Corwen! For some reason Ryan and I had to go by car (not included in the fee) to catch up with our fellow artistes in the pavilion at Corwen. He decided that he would mime a duet, 'Hywel and Blodwen'. He would sing Blodwen's part – his first performance in drag – and I was to mime Hywel, the tenor part. This duet, although rather hackneyed by now, is from an opera of the same name by Dr Joseph Parry which is very well-known to Welsh audiences. To execute this venture we had to obtain a record, which Ryan acquired from the college library. It was an old 'Master's Voice' record with a dog and an ancient gramophone on its label. We placed this sacred vintage sound on the ledge under the car's back window and raced like the Valkyries towards Corwen. It was a hot, sweltering day, and by the time we reached our destination, the treasured record had melted! It was on the verge of turning into a treacled solution, and had crumpled at the edge like a popadum. We placed it gingerly under a box in an effort to flatten it. We thought the trick had worked, but when it was placed on the turntable, it made the most horrific noise I had ever heard before rock music was invented. At least it had not cracked, and Ryan could return the brittle object secretly into the college library! Not to be daunted by this mishap, Ryan decided to sing the duet with Valerie Ffoukes, a very talented soprano from Rhosllannerchrugog who was a member of our company. This time, he was to sing Hywel's part while Valerie sang Blodwen's. The drag act, much to my relief, had gone out of the window! Valerie started singing the solo part, but Ryan was still intent upon his clowning act. He started clowning as she was singing, and the audience broke into fits of laughter. When he joined with her, poor Valerie had to start laughing as well. Many sopranos were treated to this performance in the years that were to follow. He also gave many songs a similar treatment, and his clowning had a greater appreciation when he showed, towards the end of the performance, that he actually could sing as well.

The English Society decided to produce a play by Michael Pertwee called 'Night was our Friend'. It was not as ambitious a project as 'The Lady is not for Burning', and I think Edwin chose a less demanding production for our benefit. The theme of the play, as I recollect, is rather a simple story. A young man, believed dead, returns home after being kept prisoner in Malaya, or some similar jungle-infested country. By this time, his wife has fallen in love with the local doctor or lawyer, but their amorous pranks have to desist with the husband's return. In the second act, it is rumoured that a deranged man is prowling the countryside at night, attacking innocent persons. By now of course, you will have realised, without being amateur Agatha Christies, that the deranged loner turns out to be the young husband. Planning his escape from the malaria-, snake- and guard-infested jungle has affected his 'nut'. Nocturnal prowling is a habit he cannot get rid of. However, his attempt at attacking or murdering his wife is thwarted by the timely entrance of the young lover. The lunatic husband is put in safe custody, and the young lover and the wife live happily ever after.

Ryan played the part of the returned husband, and, although it was a simpler part to play than Thomas Mendip, it cast a light on another aspect of his ability as an actor. Whereas Mendip was a verbal character, full of gusto for life, this character needed the opposite treatment — constraint. The way Ryan played the shy, quiet neurotic man who had returned from adversity gained the audience's sympathy. It was only a few controlled flashes of his eye that made the audience suspect that he might be the maniac who jumped out of hedgerows with murder on his mind. Ryan began to learn this technique of acting in a lower register during this production of Edwin's, although he never quite mastered this kind of acting for many years.

Ryan had played rugby for the college in the first year, indeed he gained the college colours in rugby and in cricket. In our second year, John Huw Evans (Huwcyn) became captain of the college rugby team. Ryan and I were very close friends of his for many years, and one could describe him, like many rugby forwards, as a gentle giant, at least in everyday life. However, as soon as he stepped over a touchline, he would show no mercy to man or mouse. Huwcyn was incredibly strong and played lock for the college team. Adam's Gwyn Roblin (WRU president in 1980) was a lecturer in our college, and more than anyone, was the greatest instigator of the game in North Wales. Mr Roblin, a very kind enthusiastic man, and the late Mr Llywelyn Rees inspired us to start a second rugby team. Since Huwcyn was the captain, John Rich and myself, both north Walians, who had hardly ever played rugby previously, volunteered to play second-row forwards for the embryo team. Because Ryan played on the wing for the first team, John Rich and I played in the same team during practice matches against Huwcyn's team. One afternoon on the college field, wittily nicknamed 'the lower plateau' by our previous principal, Huwcyn tackled me with such enormous ferocity that I lay stunned on the ground. As I counted the billionth star in the galaxy, Ryan and John Rich came up to me with mock sympathy: "Don't take it personally. Wait till tonight in the Antelope. Even if he so much as coughs in your direction, he'll apologise". Ryan had plenty of self-confidence, even on a rugby field. Sometimes one would think that he was just bloody stubborn; he would never give in. His frail body would vanish under a

54

cloud of jerseys only to bounce out through a forest of arms and legs to continue the game. 'Enough is enough' was an unknown phrase to him.

Ryan had another trait that is worth mentioning. He loved involving himself with the absurd. I know that students in general invent absurd things, but Ryan and Brian Jones, a student from the south Wales valleys a brilliant scrum-half, set up the College Marbles League. That in itself is verging on the realms of absurdity, but what made it really absurd was their attire. They dressed like American football players and trotted out, in line, into the hostel corridors, padded to the hilt. They stuffed their track-suits with foam rubber, magazines and towels, with crash helmets on their heads – just to play marbles! This was years before Monty Python was ever thought of! They took the League very seriously, and I was put on the table for taking the mick out of their actions. They invented incredible names for their teams such as the Bethesda Moonshiners, the Top-floor Misogynists and the Annex Incorruptibles. No wonder the Goon Show, featuring the zany humour of Sellers, Secombe and Milligan, was his favourite radio programme.

In the midst of all these student frivolities, one tends to forget that the primary reason for being in the college was to be taught how to teach. Not only was Ryan an actor by instinct, but he was also a teacher. I do not believe that he was even remotely academically-inclined, but in front of a classroom he had that special gift that made him a special teacher. Part of our training involved visiting a school for some months as student teachers, for what was called 'school practice'. The lecturers would visit us occasionally, and the most endowed were paid a visit by immortal beings called HMI's – Her Majesty's Inspectors. Ryan had such a visit when he did his school practice in Porthmadog (the town where Lawrence of Arabia was born, not that such information is even remotely connected), and he was regarded as a potential 'A' teacher. I attended the same main course as Ryan in English Literature and, in a mini thesis we had to write, he wrote about Thomas Hardy. Whereas I studied Welsh Literature, Ryan took Music, but often we discussed the great poets of Wales rather than the English poets. Although he did not study in Welsh, he was very familiar with the poetry of T H Parry-Williams, Robert Williams Parry and Gwenallt, and he could quote endlessly from their work.

However, all good things come to an end, and after taking our final exams, for which we were ill-prepared, we were ready to leave Bangor for the last time. Much to our disgust, one could count on the fingers of one hand the number of evenings we had stayed in 'on the books'. Two! We had spent many more on the college stage, in the cinemas, and propping up the bar of the Antelope. So much for the sweet bird of youth!

Before leaving college, we had to perform a college ritual. A student, not reluctantly I may add, would donate a particular book – *Child Psychology* by Percy Nunn. This book, which had been a source of mental agony to the majority of us for two years, would be placed on a wreath made of flowers stolen from the college garden. All the students leaving our hostel, the George, would then line up, as at a funeral. The lamenting squad would then trudge slowly to the banks of the Menai Straits, singing 'All university students are illigitimate' in a minor key. A short mock-prayer in memory of Plato and the basic concept of education would be uttered before Nunn's masterpiece was tipped gently into the water. After we had, with mock lament, watched this leafy mine of information vanish into the cold current of the straits, everyone would shout with jubilation, 'Normal College for ever'. Everyone returned home, but Ryan, myself and a few students, had to return to the college in a few weeks' time, to start work on a play to be performed at the National Eisteddfod in Caernarfon in August, 1959.

I was staying with Ryan at the Dolydd when the examination results arrived. His mother brought the inevitable envelope to Ryan's bedroom, and called me in. Gingerly Ryan opened the envelope. If his thoughts were anything like mine, he was wishing that he had worked harder! The cash register at the Antelope must have been ringing in his ears!

By some strange miracle both of us had passed. It was another day of celebration. Ryan had decided to take a further course in drama at the Central School of Speech and Drama in London, whereas I had been accepted by the Croydon Education Authority as an English teacher in New Addington. Ryan often pulled my leg that I was going to teach English in England: "It's like sending a communist to the Vatican!"

A fortnight before the National Eisteddfod at Caernarfon, all the cast assembled at the George hostel – women included! Female feet, other than those of ageing cleaners, had never before trodden the sanctity of those polished corridors. It was like seeing nuns in a monastery, or a 'monkery' as Ryan called it. It was like living in the land of the Lotus Eaters!

We worked very hard during this period. Edwin had instilled in us a love of the stage during the years, and we respected him so much as a lecturer and producer that everyone in the cast would work their fingers to the bone for him. Edwin, more than anyone, gave Ryan's acting an edge which was to help him for the rest of his acting career.

Edwin decided to produce a translation by Adam's F G Fisher of André Obey's 'Noah'. I met the late Mr Fisher a few years later when he was a Mathematics teacher at Llangefni Grammar School. He had learnt the Welsh language and was the main instigator of Theatr Fach Llangefni (the Llangefni Little Theatre), one of the few amateur theatres in Wales that is a member of the Little Theatre Guild of Great Britain. I had been cast by Edwin to play Noah. I read in the Bible that the poor gentleman died when he was 950 years old! He would have made a bomb from any life insurance company! Ryan was chosen to play Shem, Noah's son.

I suppose one could rightly describe Obey's play as a modern morality play. He has based his plot on the old biblical story. Noah finds wives for his three sons, Ham, Shem and Japheth – Naomi, Sela and Ada. With his wife he takes them on board the ark, saving them from the deluge. After sailing on an endless ocean for a very long time, Shem becomes bored, and decides to turn the others against his father. He persuades his brother Japheth, the weakest of all the passengers, to try and catch the fish that are swimming near the ark. He starts whipping the bear, Noah's favourite animal and friend, and eventually persuades the occupants of the ark that Noah is no more than a good farmer who can forecast the weather. He takes over command of the ark against his father's will and puts up a sail, so that they can sail by their own navigation rather than float across the ocean at the whim of God. Obey conveys that the desire in man, his need to rule, his desire to be a tyrant and his defiance of the Divine is carried through the deluge in the character of Shem. It is only the return of the dove with a green sprig in its beak, at the end of the fourth act, that saves the situation. However, at the end, all their affection and trust in one another has disappeared. In the last act, the different couples vanish to propagate the human race in different regions of the earth. Noah remains with his wife, dejected; even his favourite animal, the bear, turns on him and tries to maul him.

Although I had acted with Ryan in the three previous plays I have mentioned, it was the first time that I played his opposite number. The pace and conflict of the play relies on the characterisation of Shem and Noah. When I delivered a line, he knew when to pause, throw a line, or hammer it back at me. It was like playing tennis with dialogue. There were times when we could build up enormous tension; at other times the whole thing seemed to sag and become deadly boring. Perhaps it was the fact that one of us was straining to remember the lines, rather than feeling them, or perhaps we had become over-confident of our dialogue, feeling our lines too much, losing control of them. We were only inexperienced amateurs, of course, but even now, working with professional players, I sometimes see traits of the same dilemma. Years later, I heard from much better actors than myself how exhilarating it was to act opposite Ryan. Over the years he, learned how to sustain the same level of performance night after night, even when he was struggling against ill health.

Two memories remain with me from that particular production. My girlfriend during my student days was a girl named Gwen, and her father had shot a wild pigeon somewhere in Anglesey. This dead bird became a very important member of our cast. In the fourth act I had a long monologue to speak to the shot pigeon – sitting upstage, trying to prop its wilted neck between my fingers so that it would appear to be slightly alive. However, the week of the Caernarfon Eisteddfod was one of the hottest in the history of our ancient festival. By the evening of our final performance my feathered friend had began to smell to high heaven. I said to Ryan, "Ry, I don't know how the hell I'm going to manage the monologue to this pigeon; it's really high". He took the pigeon from me, smelt it, and said, "You're right, Rhydd. Speaking to that thing is like reciting poetry to a 'bird' without any teeth!"

A few minutes later after the monologue I had to take the stinking bird upstage, speak to it again, and throw it out to the wings to Huwcyn – who was playing the part of the bear, often with more ferocity than was necessary – and he was supposed to catch it. I spoke some divine lyrical lines such as, "Go white dove – seek the truth – the sign of God". I threw it out with a pass that would make Gareth Edwards despair of the human race. Huwcyn missed it and it fell to the boards with the most embarrassing 'plop' ever heard in amateur theatrical history. Ryan and the rest of the cast were in fits of laughter in the wings, not so much because I was a cumbersome actor, but a really second-rate rugby player.

After this performance, Emyr Edwards – now a lecturer at Barry Training College – wrote in his new drama magazine, "I was very impressed with the performance of John O Roberts as Robert in Anouilh's play, Alun Evans as Gwyn and Wenna Thomas as Peggy in John Gwilym Jones' play and Ryan Davies as Shem in Obey's play. These actors have an important part to play in the future of the Welsh Theatre. The ideal would be to see these young people receiving tuition in a professional Welsh Drama College".

That comment was made in 1959, and in 1976 the first course for actors in the Welsh language was started at the College of Music and Drama in Cardiff. Furthermore Bangor and Aberystwyth universities now offer Drama as a subject. Ryan was fortunate to have enrolled at the

Normal College when Edwin Williams' department was opened, and, as I mentioned earlier, he was on his way to the Central College of Drama in London.

Ryan and I had a stroke of good luck at the same Eisteddfod, because we met many members of the London Welsh Association. We met Peter Lloyd, O.B.E., who was then the Honorary Secretary of the Association, and were invited to perform in their Noson Lawen at the local cinema. Ryan was performing one of his mimes when a poodle belonging to Mati Pritchard took an interest in his silent act by barking and, eventually, joined him onstage! Undeterred by this intrusion, Ryan continued with his mime, but it became a man and dog act, much to the amusement of the audience.

John Williams, another prominent London Welshman who became a good friend of ours, asked us to perform in a private 'Noson Lawen' at the Menai Bridge home of millionaire Howel Hughes from Bogota. You can imagine the rustic eyebrows that were raised when a huge shining Rolls-Royce picked us up in front of Lloyd George's statue on Caernarfon square. We fancied that the statue winked at us. We performed in a huge parlour, accompanied by the harp, to an audience crammed with fur-coated ladies. They looked incongruous in the sweltering heat of the evening. For our trouble, we were given two cardboard cups of orange juice. Lloyd George's statue must have been trying to warn us!

Peter Lloyd took a great interest in both of us when he heard that we were coming to London to start our new careers. We also met David and Mary Richards, and Bryn and Shirley Richards. Both David and Bryn were to be close friends of Ryan and myself for many years, influencing Ryan's future career. Gwenlyn Parry and his wife Joy, whom I had known since my army days, also came to know Ryan very well, although they had just left London to teach in Caernarfonshire.

However, we bid farewell to our friend Edwin Williams and many of our college tutors. The next stop was Lewisham. I don't remember where we buried the pigeon…

# The London Welsh, a Gerund and the Albert Hall

JOHN RICH, HUWCYN, and I considered that we'd lived in London long enough to be counted as real Cockneys by the time Ryan arrived in London. We shared a flat in Burnt Ash Road, Lewisham. The flat was a genetic freak that might occur if you crossed a medieval castle with an igloo. However it was habitable on those days when John Rich was not repairing his motorbike in the kitchen, and was paradise in comparison with subsequent flats. John and Huwcyn were teaching near London Bridge and I was in Croydon. Every school day was a long trek. The location only suited the three of us on Saturdays, when we played rugby for Sidcup. Ryan's first night was spent with us in our flat. Our bedroom was more like a field than part of a house, with an enormous double bed and a single. John Rich slept in the single bed, wrapped in multiple layers of nightwear that made him look like an onion. Ryan had to sleep between Huwcyn and myself, both of us rugby forwards. Ryan talked of it often; "It was like sleeping in the middle of the Atlantic! Both of you decided to turn on your sides at the same time, one to the right, and the other to the left. I was lifted, as if on the crest of a huge wave, and then fell a few feet through space".

The following morning he went to enrol at the Central School of Speech and Drama. Like many Welsh actors before him, he could have found the thespian atmosphere of such an establishment very enticing, but not so Ryan. His love of all things Welsh led him to the London Welsh Centre in Gray's Inn Road. We had promised Peter Lloyd at the Caernarfon Eisteddfod that we would lend a constructive hand with the activities of the Centre. I took over the Welsh classes that my friends Gwenlyn Parry and his wife Joy had started. Naturally, most of the students were the children of Welsh parents who had emigrated to London and lost their language, but there was a lovely old Cockney lady at my first class. When I asked her why she wanted to learn Welsh, she replied, "Because I loves yer 'ymn singing!" I also took over the 'Aelwyd', a branch of Urdd Gobaith Cymru (the Welsh League of Youth) for young people aged 18–25. Ryan quickly joined me and was soon helping Hafina Clwyd, Howard Goodfellow, and myself to run the various activities. He was soon running a choir and a folk-dancing party.

Peter Lloyd was a health inspector in the West End, and ran the Centre in his spare-time. He had boundless energy, working till the early hours. He was a good friend to Ryan and I during our years within earshot of Bow Bells.

Peter put on a concert in the London Welsh Hall on Saturday, 10 October, 1959. Amongst the artists was Stuart Burrows, the famous international tenor. He was a teacher at Pontypridd at the time, and had won the tenor solo and the Blue Ribbon Open Competition at the National Eisteddfod in Caernarfon. He subsequently became one of Ryan's friends.

After this concert, Ryan and I had endless invitations to perform in chapels and vestries for all kinds of denominations and societies in London. During those months we ate enough cold ham and limp lettuce to give us myxomatosis. From Gray's Inn Road we darted off to Charing Cross, King's Cross, Harrow, Finchley and many other places. Perhaps you can recall the scene in the film 'Run for your Money' when the late Huw Griffith and Meredydd Edwards take Huw's harp from the pawnshop. Ryan and I re-enacted that scene frequently in those days. We were not desperate enough to have to pawn a harp, but as Ryan's harp was at his parents', we borrowed one from the London Welsh Association. We were once dashing up and down Gray's Inn Road calling for a taxi, just as the rush hour traffic was calming down. Ryan was standing on the pavement supporting a huge Grecian harp. Eventually a taxi dashed towards me, when I heard Ryan shout,

"That one's no use!"

"Why not?" I shouted back.

"You've got to get a square one".

"What do you mean? Every taxi is square."

"You'll never get this harp into a modern taxi – it won't fit."

True enough; we had to find an older model, and even then it was touch and go. Ryan would be perched on the seat with the harp on top of him, whilst I was comfortable enough. I travelled through London as if I was the impressario of Sadler's Wells. From underneath the harp's canvas cover, Ryan would mutter, "If only I had learnt to play the fiddle, the flute or the piccolo!"

In our concerts, Ryan and I sang a lot of 'penillion'. This form of singing, accompanied by the harp, is as peculiar to the Welsh as mouth music is to the Scottish Gaelic singers. In simple terms, it is the expression of poetic work in music to the counterpoint of a well-known air. The poetry has to be set in relation to the harp accompaniment. The settings that Ryan and I sang were rather old-fashioned ones we had learnt as children, and had taught to one another. A true specialist in this art wouldn't rate us very highly, but the audiences seemed to enjoy our singing.

In one 'Noson Lawen' in London, Ryan was aware that there were many non-Welsh speaking people in the audience, so he decided to give a mini-lecture on the subject of penillion-singing. I believe that his original idea was a sincere academic one, but his instructive intentions soon disappeared into thin air. He was standing onstage with yours truly on one side and the Grecian harp on the other. His speech ran something along these lines:

> Ladies and gentlemen, in a moment my friend and I will
> demonstrate the art of penillion singing. This art form, peculiar
> to the Welsh people, is as old as the hills and is sometimes called
> 'cerdd-dant' – tooth-music. ['Cerdd' means a song and 'tant'
> means string. Literally translated – the song of the string. But
> 'tant' mutates to 'dant' in this example. 'Dant' also means tooth]

His attempt at being serious wilted away. The audience started laughing, so Ryan started giving a hilarious 'talk' on the subject.

"This instrument here," he said, pointing to me, "is a harp, or an 'arp." He turned the other way and said, "Sorry, this is the harp; the other thing looks more like a tuba. Now if I sit here…" He sat on the wrong side, with the sound-board between his legs. "Sorry, wrong side," he said, before getting up and sitting on the right side. "It fits better this way. Contrary to popular belief, these pedals at the bottom of this harp are not for changing the key – one of them is the clutch; the other is the accelerator. When I pluck these strings in a preordained sequence they will make a preordained sound. This is the well-known air, 'The Ash Grove'. After a few bars, my friend usually gets drunk, but tonight he will join me, and we'll sing a melody that is different to the air that I am playing, and with a bit of luck we'll finish singing at the same time as the air comes to its end!"

He would play the harp and we would sing a poem in English. It was a well-known poem in Welsh about Madog, the son of Owain Gwynedd, who is alleged to have discovered America ages before Columbus. However, the poem had been translated literally from the Welsh so that the syntax in the English language is really up the creek:

> See them starting, ten and three
> Of quite small ships on a dark, blue sea.
> See old Madog, brave his chest,
> As captain of the ship is dressed.
> Go he is to put his foot
> Where never before a foot was put.
> This is a venture, very brave,
> But God will hold him from wave to wave.

We would sometimes try to sing serious English poetry such as Eli Jenkins' Prayer from Dylan Thomas' 'Under Milk Wood', or a poem from A E Housman's *The Shropshire Lad*: "Loveliest of trees, the cherry now/Is hung with snow along the bough…" Somehow it never caught on!

Another such evening stands out in my mind. We went to help Cyril Anthony and his brother Trefor Anthony, the famous Welsh bass, to raise money for a new roof for a London chapel. I remember that the Pembrokeshire-born actor Kenneth Griffith was also there. He recited D H Lawrence's poem 'The Ship of Death' and T S Eliot's 'The Journey of the Magi'. Trefor Anthony sang some famous operatic solos. Ryan and I performed our usual material with the harp. We were used to silver collections in concerts at home for very posh special occasions, but they were plebian in comparison with this concert. When the hat was passed round, every member of the audience deposited a cheque in it! Afterwards, Ryan, Kenneth Griffith and myself walked from the chapel towards Tottenham Court Road, one of us eating an enormous trifle with a silver spoon from the chapel!

The most enjoyable evenings of entertaining were probably when we were invited to people's homes. This was more akin to the original 'Noson Lawen', where nearly everybody 'did his bit'. We were invited to such a night at Mati Pritchard's home in Maida Vale. Mati was a very active member of the London-Welsh in those days. She was the wife of the late chaired poet Caradog Pritchard, and was at that time a sub-editor with the *Daily Telegraph*. That night we also met the famous Welsh harpist, Anne Griffiths, and her sister Mari Griffiths who now works in BBC Wales' Presentation Department. Both of them became very close friends of ours in the years ahead. As mentioned earlier, apart from taking a few lessons from Nansi Richards, Ryan was self-taught on the national instrument. Mati was so intrigued by this that she invited a Russian harpist, Maria Korchinska, to listen to him. Eventually the strange lady arrived, wearing more necklaces, brooches and rings than the white lady of Banbury Cross. She looked exactly as if she had stepped from between the covers of Doctor Zhivago! She listened intently as he played. Ryan stopped, and waited apprehensively for her verdict. After a dramatic pause that even Stanislavsky himself would have been proud of, she turned to Ryan and said, "You are a very interestink young man, but you cannot play ze harp".

Through Mati Wyn Pritchard's influence, she took an absorbing interest in our little act. We were introduced to a very kind and very beautiful lady, Isabella Wallich who owned a recording company under the label Delyse. She invited Ryan and I to make an EP of our singing. The record was called 'Welsh Fireside Song'. We were given our first copy at the London Welsh Rugby Club, of all places! It is probably the worst example of singing to the harp that was ever recorded but, to us at that time, it was the greatest revolving object since the invention of the wheel. It is still played occasionally on radio request programmes, but this will give you an indication of its sales value. Five years ago Ryan gave me a cheque for the copyright royalites (including a strange clause called 'mechanicals'), to the value of twenty-six pence! To add insult to injury, he'd forgotten to give it to me for such a long period that it had become invalid.

The record included six songs, three on either side, ranging from a love poem by Sir John Morris-Jones to a lament to Hedd Wyn, the shepherd poet who was killed in Flanders during the first World War.

Anne Griffiths had won the Premier Prix Conservatoire de Paris a few months prior to our meeting, and she condescended to play the harp for us. We felt very honoured by her gesture and decided to give Anne a treat. We decided to take her out to the West End to see a film called 'Once more with Feeling'. The film was chosen out of the blue, but its theme turned out to be rather ironic for the occasion. It starred Yul Brunner as an eccentric orchestral conductor. I still remember one of his lines: "I don't play Rimsky-Korsakov – I beat him". His leading lady in the film was Kay Kendall, the brilliant film comedienne, in her last performance before her tragic death. She played Yul Brunner's wife in the film and was also a member of his orchestra. What instrument did she play? The harp! In one scene, the husband and wife have a domestic quarrel in which he smashes his wife's harps into smithereens. I am sure that the 'prop' harps were made of papier-mâché, but you can imagine the effect it had on Anne, who had dedicated her life to this heavenly instrument. Ryan and I could feel her wince during that scene!

Most of our performances were in chapel halls, and were not even remotely connected with financial gain. The maximum fee was five pounds, and after paying the taxi driver for conveying ourselves and the harp to and fro, we were left with two pounds – one pound each! However, the moment of truth arrived; we were invited to perform at the ICI's Annual Dinner. We never quite understood why the titanic chemical industry should be interested in such folk items as we could give them, but I believe the president and vice-president that year were Welsh. We were to be paid twenty pounds for our performance – twenty whole pounds! We arrived at a very posh hotel in the centre of London. We were met by a uniformed gentleman wearing a top hat who, upon seeing the heavenly instrument, called for two porters to carry it into the hotel. Ryan and I walked behind them thinking that someone would pop out from behind the bamboo tree in the foyer to present us with an Oscar. We informed the receptionist that we were the artists who were to entertain in the Imperial Chemical Industry's Annual Dinner. The receptionist wasn't the least bit impressed, and having checked her list, she informed us – much to our horror – that we should have been there the previous evening! Ryan and I had a hell of a row, and carried the harp in silence all the way back to Gray's Inn Road. By this time Ryan and I shared a flat near King's Cross. It was the flattest flat that one could ever imagine. Even a self-respecting mouse would have turned its nose up at it. After our first and last row ever, we returned to speaking terms and started imagining what we would have been doing at that moment *had* we received the enormous fee. The tasteless coffee that we were drinking in cracked mugs became champagne in sparkling glasses. Ryan spoke to the imaginary doorman as if he were our personal valet, and invited the sexy receptionist to the poshest posh club in London! In our imaginary exploits we spent the twenty pounds ten times over.

In those days the London Welsh Association established one of the best amateur drama groups ever to act in the Welsh language. Its success can be attributed to one man, Adam's Reg Evans. Reg was a quiet, gentle person who was a history teacher. His attitude to drama was very professional and, apart from Edwin Williams, he was Ryan's greatest influence as a stage actor. When Reg died on 16 July 1977, Marie Vaughan Jones (a member of his company) wrote in his obituary in the *London Welshman*, "Many in London-Welsh circles and outside owe their knowledge of drama to him and remember his patient and courteous direction always to attain perfection".

He worked his stage movements out carefully, giving them motivation, but could readjust if an actor had good reasons to make changes. This was the kind of atmosphere that Ryan liked to work in. In 1960 the company won the drama prize at the National Eisteddfod in Cardiff. The company produced a satirical comedy by Tom Richards, who was a news editor with BBC Wales until his retirement a few years ago. The title of the play in Welsh is 'Y Cymro Cyffredin' – 'The Ordinary Welshman'. The play was set in an advertising office. One of the characters in the play sets the scene –

> My name is Tom Bowen. I work for an advertising agency in the capital city, and our work is to prepare adverts, mostly for the newspaper – but of course, by now, for the TV. Everyone has to win his bread and butter one way or another. We have been looking for an ordinary person; that is more or less the same as looking for a honest person. Of course, the ordinary person is just a number of figures on a piece of paper, the average statistics of the whims and feelings of people.
>
> Although they have been looking everywhere in Wales for a person that answers to these 'average statistics', they discover that such a person works under the same roof – the office handyman.
>
> According to their 'average statistics', these are some of the attributes of the ordinary Welshman. His name would be John Jones; his favourite lunch, fish and chips. For his tea, he would have salmon paste on toast. He would smoke ten cigarettes every day and like his pint of beer, but he would drink it in halves. In the ordinary Welshman's mind there is something

degrading in a full pint; the ordinary Welshman is no drunkard.
He does the pools every week, has heard of Owain Glyndwr,
but thinks he lives next door to Thomas Charles, the 18th
century reformist! He has heard of Daniel Owen, the Welsh
novelist, but is not quite sure whether he wrote the novel
'Rhys Lewis', or that Rhys Lewis wrote 'Daniel Owen'. That
statistical fact is the same as assuming that the average
Englishman is not quite sure whether Charles Dickens wrote
'Oliver Twist' or that Oliver Twist wrote 'Charles Dickens'.

More statistical facts are revealed and as the plot develops we find that the office handyman, John Jones, conforms to most, if not all, the data they have gathered. The advertising agency sell all their products using John James as a yardstick of public whims and needs. By the end of the play, John Jones the ordinary Welshman becomes so extraordinary that he is no longer ordinary. Ryan played the part of John Jones, and had outstanding success. This was the first time Ryan had played in the Prince of Wales Theatre in Cardiff. The adjudicator John Ellis-Williams said, "The London-Welsh company gave us one of the most polished productions I have seen. The performances of Ryan Davies as John Jones and Ieuan Davies as David Howells will be remembered for a long time".

Ieuan Davies, who is now a producer with HTV, was a brilliant comedy actor. The pair of them together could get any audience to laugh. Ieuan has contributed much to Welsh television from behind the camera, but the audience has lost a first-class actor in front of it. We had established a new 'Noson Lawen' party from amongst the young London-Welsh as we had done in college. We presented our first performance at the City Hall, Cardiff. Our friend Gwenlyn Parry came to help us, and although we had rehearsed our acts in London, we wouldn't let on about the nature of the sketches. Every time he enquired, we would tell him that 'everything would be all right on the night'. By the time the curtain went up, Gwenlyn was virtually a nervous wreck. When the curtain did go up, Ryan went to the piano and played a few bars of the Welsh national anthem. The audience were a bit wary of this unusual custom but eventually a thousand people stood up. At that moment Ryan played a different bright tune and a chorus of young people came on telling them all to sit down! A thousand people had been hoodwinked at the same time, and from that point on we had them in the palms of our hands.

I am not sure to what extent the Central School of Speech and Drama influenced him. I know that he took part in two college productions, playing Noah in an English translation of Obey's 'Noah', and Jimmy Porter in John Osborne's 'Look Back in Anger'. He was strongly influenced by the writings of the Russian actor and producer Constantin Stanislavsky – *The Actor Prepares* and *My Life in Art*. Ryan came home to the flat one evening and told me a story he had heard in a lecture.

Stanislavsky was the son of a prosperous farmer in Russia before the revolution. At dinner one evening he boasted that he could take his father's most ill-tempered horse out of the stable. His father took him up on his boast. Fearing that his brothers and sisters would regard him as a coward, the more unpleasant their revelations became, the more obstinate he became, and said, "I am not afraid. I will lead him out". He was taken to the courtyard in the darkness and left there. In the stygian conditions he became afraid, and imagined the wild horse in the stable. He stays in the unfriendly courtyard seeing the cosy firelight through the windows, making the hostile darkness darker. He is too afraid of the horse, and his conscience will not allow him to lie his way back to the hearth. He hears something moving in the darkness. His fear increases, but he gets enormous relief when he discovers that it is his friendly dog. There is strength in numbers, and much of the fear vanishes. A coachman arrives, and the boy gets an idea. He decides to ask the coachman if he can take the wild horse out of the stable, knowing that the coachman will refuse. Then he can safely return to the house, tell his father, and his honour will be intact. The darkness becomes friendly all of a sudden, but not for long. The horse, which the coachman has brought into the courtyard, goes beserk and races madly around the yard; fear returns again. Recently I found the passage Ryan was referring to in a chapter under the title 'Struggle with Obstinacy' in Stanislavsky's book *My Life in Art*. This is how he ends the story about Voronoy, the wild horse:

> I don't exactly remember what happened after. I stood near the front door and rang the bell. The doorman came out and let me in. Of course, he must have been waiting for me. In the doorway of the lobby flashed the figure of my father; the governess looked down from the staircase. I sat down on a chair in the lobby without removing my coat. My entrance into the house was so unexpected to myself that I could not decide what to do – to continue in my obstinacy and to affirm that I had only come in to warm myself in order to go out to Voronoy again, or to confess my cowardice and surrender. I was so dissatisfied with myself for my smallness of spirit that I was already ashamed of the role of hero. Besides, there was nobody to enjoy my performance. All of them seemed to have forgotten about me. "So much the better. I will also forget. I will remove my coat, wait a little while, and then go into the parlour." And that is what I did. Nobody asked me anything about Voronoy. It must be that they had agreed not to.

The story in itself is rather simple but the young boy in the situation had experienced so many emotions in a short time. He had boasted, felt cowardice, conflict, fear, warmth in the dog's company, relief, terror, relief, and anticlimax, with hardly a word uttered. Ryan felt that this little story was a good introduction to understanding Stanislavsky's method acting. It is so important for an actor to experience the emotions that he has to project on the stage or in front of a camera.

I had become engaged to Gwen, a fellow student, before I left college, but things didn't turn out too well. We broke up, and she gave the engagement ring to Ryan to return to me. He gave it to me in the flat one Saturday morning, and I was going to make a romantic gesture such as throwing it into the Thames. However, after we had discussed our financial position it was decided that such flamboyance would be the act of a madman. We decided to flog it in Trafalgar Square. Although I had lost the receipt, we received a small fortune for it. We became quite merry that afternoon in the West End, and ended up in a cinema watching Charlie Chaplin. Ryan was greatly influenced by the veteran's acting, and there were strong traces of the master's antics in Ryan's work. That evening we went to Euston to meet Irene, who came up from Wales for the weekend, and then we took Anne Evans, who is now a famous opera singer, with us to Battersea fun park the following Sunday. Well, if something's got to end, it might as well end with a flourish!

We still wrote songs together in those days, and the trio from the Normal College, Ryan, Phil and Ifor, were invited to sing at the St David's Day concert at the Albert Hall produced by Peter Morley Jones. At the end of the concert I remember Ryan saying to Peter and his assistants, "Thank you for inviting us, and I would also like to thank Albert for the loan of his hall".

During the interval in this concert Ryan and I were invited to be introduced to Her Royal Highness Princess Alexandra by Lord Aberdare, who was President of the London Welsh Association that year. We were lined up on a red carpet amongst the dignitaries, having been instructed just to touch her fingertips and not to give a rattling good handshake. Ryan was in front of me. Now at that time I was teaching Welsh to Lord Aberdare. I was his tutor, mind you, not his teacher. She hardly said a word to Ryan, and he disappeared. However when I was introduced, Lord Aberdare informed her that I was his Welsh tutor.

"What kind of a language is it?" she asked me.

It was rather difficult to explain in approximately twenty seconds the grammatical structure of one of Europe's oldest languages. If any self-respecting linguist had heard my answer he would have jumped off the balcony into the well of the Albert Hall. In a moment of assumed nonchalance I said, "Grammatically it is similar to French. Phonetically it is like German". Then she stumped me completely and asked, "How many gerunds has it got?"

I knew that the gerund was important in German but, to be truthful, I didn't even know if Welsh had a gerund let alone how many. Not wishing to let myself down as a tutor or to show my ignorance, and being an ardent Welshman, I replied,

"Three, your Highness," with as much conviction as a prophet talking about the past.

Ryan was waiting around the corner.

"What did she say to you?" he asked.

"Never mind that," I answered. "Do you know how many gerunds there are in the Welsh language?"

"Gerunds? What do you mean?"

"You know – gerunds. The things you have in grammar – things to do with the condition of the verb, or something."

"Ah! I know what you mean. I know what a gerund is. We had one in the back garden but the wheels came off."

The first year in London had been a very exciting one. On Sunday evenings we would visit Anne Evans' mother, Mrs Nellie Evans, who would mother and feed us. Ryan and Anne would go to the piano and sing duets till the early morning. Salad days!

Ryan completed his course at the Central School of Speech and Drama. When this was made known to Mr Gerallt Lewis, headmaster of Shirley Primary School in Croydon, he invited Ryan to join his staff.

# Teaching, Laski and a Wedding

WHEN RYAN CAME to teach in Croydon, Huwcyn was also teaching in the same school. I was teaching there already, and our friend Dan Roberts, now a representative with the NUT, came to teach there, too. Writing to me a few years ago, Gerallt Lewis said that a certain Local Education Officer who was a bit of a wag told him that all adverts in the press from that term on should read as follows –

"From now on, the Croydon Education Committee will have to insist that any future appointment at St John's [Gerallt's School] will include in the advertisement: Welsh need not be spoken".

The four of us shared an enormous flat in a very posh part of South Croydon. It was a palace in comparison with the rabbit hutch Ryan and I had shared in King's Cross. Huwcyn and I played rugby for Sidcup RFC, and many old college friends joined us: Peter Duggan, who now teaches at Ardwyn School, Aberystwyth; Gareth Evans, Colin Jones, Tom Davies, Tom Prosser, and many more. The influence of Gwyn Roblin and Llew Rees, our college lecturers, could be seen every Saturday afternoon on the rugby fields of Surrey. From the first team to the Extra B's, although wearing Sidcup jerseys, half of every team wore the green and red stockings of the Normal College! Ryan gave up playing rugby because he had started a children's choir at the school and supervised a rehearsal every Saturday morning. He held a concert at the school and raised enough money to take his choir to the International Eisteddfod at Llangollen. They did not qualify to appear at the pavilion, but Ryan and Gerallt took the children to Betws-y-Coed, Snowdonia, and Caernarfon. Ryan was in his element with his choir, and they enjoyed themselves despite not winning. 'If at first you don't succeed, try, try again.' They would be back the following year.

Although miles away in Croydon, we were still involved with the London Welsh Association; the Welsh classes, the Welsh League of Youth, and the Drama Society. We started preparing for the Rhos National Eisteddfod of 1961. Reg Evans decided to produce a play called 'The Offshore Island' by Margharita Laski. This play had caused quite a controversy when it had been televised. In those days, there seemed to be more awareness and fear that we were on the verge of a nuclear holocaust. I was asked to translate this play into Welsh.

The play is set in a post-nuclear war farmhouse. A mother, Rachel Verney, and her two children James and Mary have managed to survive a nuclear war. The only other survivor is a fisherman, Martin, who had managed to walk upstream to the farm where the radiation had diminished, having been washed away by the water. Martin and Rachel Verney copulate without any true affection for one another, just like animals, in order to keep the human race alive. At the end of the first act, a crowd of Americans arrive on a rescue mission. Martin goes into hiding, and the Americans are ignorant of his survival. Captain Charles, the leader of the group becomes fond of Rachel Verney, and for the first time in ten years she finds someone of compatible intellect to talk to. When she asks him why America bombed Britain he replies, "Little countries were bombed for all kinds of reasons". To them Britain was just an 'offshore island'. At the beginning of the last act another rescue mission arrives; this time Russian. Captain Baltinsky – the leader of the Russian group – and Captain Charles make a pact. They decide to drop a small atomic bomb on the farm to neutralize the land with radiation so that one side can't take advantage of it against the other. They are going to kill James' land, of which he was so proud. The Americans offer to rescue them and take them to America. They jump at the offer, but soon discover that they would not be free in the new land. They would be placed in concentration camps because they had been exposed to radioactivity. They remembered what had happened when the sow had littered. She had given birth to piglets that had two heads. This is one of the after-effects that gamma rays have on the chromosome structure. The gruesome story leads up to this scene, where Captain Charles, unaware of the fisherman's existence, thinks that the son is his mother's lover, and shoots him. Ryan played the part of the son James.

## THE OFFSHORE ISLAND

*Rachel:* I've enjoyed civilisation too much to be happy in a new stone age. But for ten years I've been free from guilt. I've lived at no one's expense. The things that have been valuable have been truly valuable, not a matter of making money and spending it, showing that you've made it and spent it. I've had no part in hurting and killing for words. I've lived in peace with my family.

*Mary:* I shall never have a family.

*Bayford:* Cheer up, now. You don't want to take it like that. There's other things in life besides kids. You take it from me, they're nothing but a blasted nuisance. And when there's no danger of having kids, why, you wouldn't believe the fun you can have instead.

*Charles* Sergeant, ready for take-off?

*Bayford:* OK. *(He turns to go, then pauses)* Might as well take your stuff along, while I'm about it.

*(He picks up the coat and the bag, and as he goes he winks at Charles)* Whatever else don't go, be a pity to leave this behind. *(He goes)*

*Charles (To Rachel):* He put it crudely, but what he said was true. There's lots of people never have any children.

*Rachel:* Or any freedom?

*Charles:* You don't call this freedom?

*Rachel:* Yes. Freedom is what it is.

*Charles:* You'll be safe there, you won't have to worry where your next meal's coming from. And there's other young people. *(To*

*Rachel, about Mary):* You want to make her look at it like that.
*Rachel:* And how do I look at it?
*Charles:* It's not so bad in the reservations, really it isn't. They're properly inspected – why, there was an article in *Time* magazine only a short while ago and it all looked grand. There's lots of people – and you said you were lonely. *(Pleading)* You said you wanted people to talk to.
*Rachel:* I wanted more than that.
*Charles (Angry and brutal):* Well you can have that too. I wasn't good enough for you, was I, but no doubt some husky CP will be delighted to oblige.
*James (Swinging round):* My mother doesn't need you, or any CP either. She's got a better man – *(He stops, appalled)*
*Charles (With slow menace):* Just what do you mean? *(James's mouth works. He tries to get out words, then twists his face into a travesty of a smile)*
*James:* What do you think I mean? How do you think we manage?
*Charles:* You scum.
*(He hits out at James, who half falls, but looks up, daring him)*
You filthy little animal.
*(He pulls out his gun and shoots James, who falls, then looks to Rachel)*

I remember one occasion when we were rehearsing the scene I have just quoted. We were being put through our paces in the London Welsh Hall one evening. We knew our words, but did not have costumes or a set. It was just an ordinary rehearsal, except for one prop we were using for the first time. Iwan Thomas (now a newscaster with BBC Wales), who played one of the Americans, brought a revolver with him. The scene you have just read became alive because all the actors were aware of this frightening implement. When Ieuan Davies (Captain Charles) 'shot' Ryan that evening, the true pathos of Laski's powerful play appeared. In that memorable rehearsal I wept for the inhumanity of the human race. We performed the play quite a few times subsequently, with costumes, make-up, sets and audience, but that particular scene was never quite the same as it had been the evening Iwan brought the gun.

Dr John Gwilym Jones was the adjudicator when we presented the play at the Rhos National Eisteddfod, and once more the company was victorious. Reg Evans was also presented with the Meredydd Edwards drama cup for the festival's best drama production.

During rehearsals of 'Offshore Island', Ryan, Iwan Thomas, Ieuan Davies and myself were invited to Marghanita Laski's home in Hampstead. We were all very excited by the invitation. Ryan and I knew nothing about our hostess. We need not have worried; Iwan, then a civil servant had looked up her credentials in *Who's Who*. As we travelled in the tube towards Hampstead, he informed us that she was the daughter of Harold Laski, the famous economist, who had balanced the sheets for Britain during the Second World War. She was a regular contributor to the famous radio programme 'The Brains Trust'. We knew that she was the author of 'The Offshore Island' and Iwan informed us that she had also written a book called *The Chaise Longue*. Iwan kept on feeding us more information and our admiration for the lady grew increasingly as we rattled on from station to station.

Marghanita Laski turned out to be an extremely loveable person, and we were given a princely welcome in her home. As we drank gins and martinis like a nest of cuckoo-chicks, she informed us that she had written 'The Offshore Island' as a commission from the BBC. She had completed the manuscript but was so unhappy with the end product that she had thrown it into the bin, and returned the commission fee to the BBC. As fate would have it, a certain J B called to see her before the garbage collector's arrival, and she retrieved her literary work from the bin. J B read the script and persuaded her that her play was a good one. The four of us were nodding our head like four rams, approving of J B's divine intervention, saving the script from the bowels of the LCC's garbage dump. But who the hell was J B? We felt rather stupid when it dawned on us that J B was none other than J B Priestley. Who else? Priestley was apparently a close friend of the family and we knew a little about his literary prowess.

Unfortunately for us, she stopped discussing her play and J B. For some reason she turned her discussion to French literature, quoting from Racine and Voltaire – in French! If our knowledge of Priestley had been limited, we were now well out of our depth. For a quarter of an hour we kept nodding like nincompoops. Somehow Gerard Manley Hopkins was mentioned and I managed to bring 'cynghanedd' into the discussion. At last, I thought, we were playing on our own ground. No way! Marghanita Laski knew as much about cynghanedd as we did, and talked about Dafydd ap Gwilym, the 14th century poet, as if he were a long-lost friend! Like a flash Ryan saved the situation. To this living day I remember his line:

"Talking about 'cynghanedd', is that a harpsichord?"

"Yes," she replied. "Can you play?"

He walked to a harpsichord in the corner, opened the lid and played. We sang a duet to her of the poetry in the strict metre we had been discussing, and she was very thrilled. Later we sent her an LP record, called 'The Heart and Voice of Wales', again on the Delyse label, on which we sang one song. After we had sung our duet, Ryan sang and played for the rest of the evening. To our relief it turned out to be more of an 'entertaining' rather than an 'intellectual' one. Earlier, a beautiful girl called Lydia had come into the room. She was Marghanita Laski's daughter, a student at Oxford. According to Iwan's research she had stated in the press a few weeks earlier that she would willingly sleep with any man if she found him interesting. It was a rather daring statement to make in those less promiscuous days but as we stood on the station on our way home, one of us said out of the blue, "I wonder how interesting is 'interesting'?"

The company was invited to perform 'The Offshore Island' at the Welsh National Drama Festival in Llangefni. Because of the delicate theme of the play it was the first Welsh language play to be censored. No-one under the age of eighteen was allowed to see it. When this was announced in the press our audience swelled considerably. One old farmer ordered six more tickets when he read the poster. Perhaps most Welsh people are not puritans by nature. It is probably a doctrine that has been thrust upon us!

In April 1961, Ryan and Irene were married at Llanrhaeadr-ym-Mochnant. It was a very memorable day, with relations and friends from far and wide. His best man was Brian Jones, his school friend. They lived in the flat for a while but soon they had their home near the school. Gerallt Lewis, his headmaster, tells a story in the letter he sent me –

> Back at school, everything was geared for the eleven plus in January, but after that, music did not play a secondary role. The school needed a new musical play. There weren't any suitable. Over cups of tea at Barmouth Road, Shirley, where Ryan and Irene lived, Ryan and myself decided to write our own. I was to write the words, Ryan the music. The children had done well in the eleven plus examination. 85% had won free places at Grammar Schools. The timetable from January to July was to be flexible. After assembly, where Ryan played the accompaniment to the hymns, always repeating the last verse in true Welsh spirit, the older children, instead of doing a solid hour of Maths, enjoyed learning the songs for the musical to be performed in April. 24 hours after the words of a song were written, Ryan had the music ready. An Ivor Novello style of song was sometimes chosen. Other times, it was perhaps influenced by Gilbert and Sullivan. Other times it was pure Ryan. The children loved them all. 'Paradise Island' was ready in time.

The musical play for juniors, 'Paradise Island', was published by the Oxford University Press. It was the first time his music was published. In the same letter that Gerallt sent me when I was doing some research for his biography, he relates another story about school life:

The then-Ministry of Education sent a party of inspectors to St John's School, Shirley, just outside Croydon, for a full inspection of the school which was done every five years by an efficient Ministry. The Chief Inspector chose to inspect Ryan Davies' class for a Science lesson. This was the only subject Ryan did not enjoy taking. The lesson was for 1.45–2.45. I broke the news to Ryan immediately. Mr Johns mentioned it at 12.00 noon. Apparatus was hurriedly borrowed from a nearby secondary school for a lesson on expansion of metals. At lunchtime Ryan and myself, in consultation, prepared for action. After the lesson Mr Johns came to my room. 'I am worried about Mr Ryan Davies.' I was about to take the blame for any mishap, but before he could speak, Mr Johns said, 'I have never seen anything like it in all my experience. Not only were the children's eyes popping. So were mine. He must take charge of Science teaching throughout the school'. I kept quiet. Mr Johns continued with his admiration. I knew Ryan had put on a performance. This was one of many of his gifts.

As if teaching and training the school choir and cricket team wasn't enough, he joined the West Wickham opera society, where he took the leading tenor role in such musicals as 'The Mikado', 'The Pirates of Penzance' and 'Merry England'. I remember going to see him take the part of Nanki-Poo in 'The Mikado'. The character of Nanki-Poo, the son of the Mikado of Japan disguised as a wandering minstrel, was ideal for Ryan. He loved singing such songs as his opening number:

A wandering minstrel I –
A thing of shreds and patches,
Of ballads, songs and snatches,
And dreamy lullabies.
My catalogue is long,
Through every passion ranging
And to your humours changing
I tune my supply changing.

He gave a brilliant performance in this role, and in retrospect I believe the character of Nanki Poo tells us much about Ryan himself.

Naturally, with his new role as a young husband venturing into domestic life, I did not see him as often, but we continued to visit the London Welsh. I was asked to translate Brandon Thomas' famous farce 'Charlie's Aunt' into Welsh, to enter the drama competition at the Llanelli National Eisteddfod. This play was chosen with Ryan in mind to play the lead Fancourt Babberley. We decided to enter the one-act competition with our dear friend Gwenlyn Parry's new play 'The Little Hawthorn' – 'Y Ddraenen Fach'. I still don't know how we managed everything with only seven days in a week.

# Charlie's Aunt, Television and Bethan Mair

WHEN 'CHARLIE'S AUNT' was performed at the Llanelli National Eisteddfod, a well-known Welsh drama critic Adam's John Ellis Williams remarked that to perform such a play at the Eisteddfod was like singing 'Have a banana' at the Edinburgh Festival! John became a good friend in the years ahead, but I did not quite understand what he was getting at in his rather whimsical remark. I suppose that he was referring to the dandiacal background of the play – the Oxford College – that was so alien to Welshness. At the same time, many Welsh students have been to Oxford; indeed, one might say that Jesus College Oxford was a home from home for Welshmen. However, I regard Thomas' play as the classic amongst farces, and it was a first class vehicle for Ryan's acting talent. The entrances and exits have been worked out brilliantly, and have to be executed with the precision of a watch to give the play its full deserved performance. Performing this play gave Ryan an edge to his timing which had always been good. Although I was acting in the play the minor part of Mr Spetigue, my big problem was translating it into the Welsh language. Even before I had set to my task, cynics were asking me how I intended translating the immortal line, 'I'm Charlie's aunt from Brazil, where the nuts came from'. I was travelling down from Croydon with Ryan and we started discussing this line. Translating it literally was simple, but in a Welsh context it loses its humour completely. Somewhere between Clapham Junction and Victoria we decided to change the old lady's country of residence. The nearest country to Brazil of any Welsh significance was Patagonia in Argentina where a Welsh colony had been founded nearly a century previously. So we invented a line which translated back into English read, 'I'm Charlie's aunt from Patagonia, where the foreign Welsh ride horses'. When it was performed for the first time in the prelim for the competition at the Cripplegate theatre in London, the line went down a treat with the audience. Even those cynics who had sat through one-and-a-half acts waiting for Ryan's delivery of the famous line hooted with merriment, and some of the audience clapped! The adjudicator was Edwin Williams, our former college lecturer; not that this made much difference. Knowing Edwin, he was probably more critical of both our performances, as we were his old students.

After the first performance at the Cripplegate, our friends David and Mary Richards held a party to celebrate the occasion. Dr Terry James (the well-known conductor, now a musical arranger in Hollywood) and Ryan were sitting at the piano. I started reciting a passage from Charles Dickens' 'A Tale of Two Cities': "It was an age of reason – it was an age of foolishness..." Terry and Ryan started playing the French National Anthem, working out variations on the theme, to fit my monologue. That was one of the amazing things about Ryan. A few hours previously, he had been Charlie's Aunt; now he was a pianist and a musician.

Our record 'The Heart and Voice' was favourably received in the national magazine, *The Gramophone*. I did not think we deserved it. It was the usual tear-jerking Welsh stereotype – miners singing through fields of daffodils on their way to work; women in tall hats eating laverbread and collecting cockles! The sooner this sentimental junk flows down the Taff the better.

On 3 March, 1962, Ryan and myself were invited to sing in the St David's Day concert at the Albert Hall. In the first half, we sang two songs that we had composed with piano accompaniment, and in the second half we did our usual harp stint. That year marked the fiftieth anniversary of the Urdd. The director, Peter Morley Jones, had arranged a finale where all the artists stood or sat onstage as if we were in a youth camp with a camp log fire burning in the foreground. Just before this final item, famous Welsh athletes such as Cliff Morgan and Carwyn James had been introduced to the audience. We all had to sing a well-known camping action-song. Ryan, myself and a Welsh second-row forward stood next to one another like the old Oxo advert, or – little, large, and huge. During the verse he'd whisper to us, "What's the next chorus?" We whispered back, "Up and down, up and down". Fifty people on the stage bent and heaved their bodies. During the next verse he'd whisper the same question. We replied, "Turn and turn". Everyone twisted their bodies. On the last verse, "What's the next chorus?"

"In and out, in and out…" we replied.

"OK lads, I'm with you this time!"

Ryan and I nearly collapsed with laughter in front of the huge audience.

We also won at the Llanelli National Eisteddfod with Gwenlyn Parry's one-act play 'The Little Hawthorn' as well as 'Charlie's Aunt'. It was a kind of dramatic grand slam amongst amateur playwrights. His play was based on an incident that occurred during the first war when the British and the Germans had a truce on Christmas Day and played football. A few weeks ago I heard on television that a film director is about to make a feature film based on the same story. Huwcyn had appeared as the bear in 'Noah', and as a Russian soldier whose only line was "We are leaving" in Russian in 'The Offshore Island'. In Gwenlyn's play he played the part of a German soldier whose only line is "Merry Christmas" in German before being shot! We never found out how good Huwcyn was at learning lines.

It was during the Llanelli Eisteddfod that television producers started taking a serious interest in Ryan as an actor and performer. From then on, both of us travelled from London to Cardiff to do small pieces for the BBC or TWW. We could have put Intercity on its feet.

Although Ryan derived most pleasure from the stage in those days, and probably for the rest of his career, he nevertheless developed a great interest in radio and television. Gwenlyn, although still living in Caernarfon, and David Richards, devised a radio programme, 'The Voices of London'. The programmes were introduced by Alun Williams, the Welsh globetrotter, humorist, commentator, and the best-known broadcaster ever to come from our country. He introduced us: "Ryan and Rhydderch, two pillars of the London Welsh Society, and when I say pillars, I don't mean caterpillars!"

It was the first time we met Alun in the flesh. Ryan and Alun were to become very close friends in future years.

The person who helped Ryan and I to take an interest in television was Adam's Aneirin Talfan Davies, above anyone. At that time he was Assistant Head of Programmes for BBC Wales. We first met him when he was scripting the Albert Hall concerts. He is a man of great literary talent and an astute critic who gave many young people their first chance in what was then the new world of television.

In the musical world we still composed together, and our songs were more 'with it' than our earlier efforts. Ryan again established a trio called The Three Taffs. They made a record for Delyse around February 1964 (EDP229). The other two members were Ryan's cousin, Alun Davies, and Bryn Richards who now works for BBC Wales.

> "The group's ambition is to introduce into Welsh singing a new international flavour on the lighter side while still retaining harmonic beauty and sincerity that is characteristic of Welsh singing".
> *Record Retailer and Music Industry News*, 20 February, 1964

However, long before this, Aneirin Talfan Davies had approached David Richards through the London Welsh Association asking him to produce a 'Noson Lawen' for television. David approached Ryan and myself, and it was decided that we would try to write a musical revue instead. It was the first of its kind in the Welsh language and was called 'Gwanwyn yn y Ddinas' ('Spring in the City'). It was a comparatively simple theme. I have dug up the script and the first shot or picture is described:

> Wide-angle of Buck Palace scene, through railings pull back to
> wide-angle including sentry-box – and track into medium shot
> Ryan thro' railings.

Ryan was a Welsh guardsman on duty outside the palace. After stamping
out a stub that he had been slyly smoking cupped in his hand, he breaks
into song. It was a humorous song about the various characters of fame
and renown that go through the gates of Buckingham palace. Obviously
the scope was endless! Did Mr Marples really ride a bike in those days?
The little Welsh guardsman gets fed-up with his lot and starts daydreaming.
With two of his mates from The Three Taffs he imagines that they meet
three young girls in the park, and in his mind's eye, they have a gay old
time romping around London. Like all dreams, it fades away, bringing us
back to the lonely guardsman, busby and all, in his sentry box.

> The London Welsh Association Aelwyd talent proved a week
> ago just how right I have been all along. Their 'Gwanwyn yn y
> Ddinas' late one Wednesday night was a gem of a programme.
> It showed how, if a real effort is made, something genuinely
> Welsh can be translated to the sophisticated TV idiom with
> complete aplomb. This is not to say, of course, that it offered
> any kind of challenge to TWTWTW or the Black and White
> Minstrels. In content, it was lightweight judged by top
> standards. But in terms of presentation, it pointed the way and
> this is something that the London-Welsh so rarely do, unless it
> be pointing the way backwards.
> Gareth Picton Evans, *London Welshman*, April 1963

It was produced by our friend David Richards and Peter Morley Jones
(who still produces the St David's Festival at the Royal Albert Hall).
Naturally, we knew very little if anything about television in those days
and Aneirin Talfan asked Jack Williams (now Head of Light Entertainment
at BBC Wales) to direct the revue. I met Jack for the first time at the
LWA hall when he came down to a rehearsal. I wasn't to know that at the

time, but Jack, more than anyone, was to encourage and assist Ryan and myself in the new world of television.

Acting in front of a camera is so different to the stage; it is a different art entirely. In many ways, it demands much more discipline in one's acting. Evidently, the stage is a continuous wide-angle – the picture contained within the proscenium arch – whereas television is the medium of the close-up. It therefore needs much more sensitive acting; a look or gesture that may appear natural onstage may be so magnified by the sensitivity of a tight lens that it would look very unnatural on the television set. Ryan, who tended to overact on the stage, had much to learn about this new technique. Indeed, it was a weakness that he did not quite eradicate for many years.

'Spring in the City' was recorded on 24 March, 1963 in Studio A, Cardiff, and although we thought it a reasonable first attempt, the BBC's response was rather negative.

On 16 January, 1965, Ryan and Irene's first child was born, a daughter named Bethan Mair. On the day of her christening I was greatly honoured; I was asked be her godfather. Only two such honours have ever been bestowed upon me in my life. I was asked to be a godfather to David and Mary Richards' daughter, also called Bethan, and to my Pembrokeshire friends Glyn and Penny Rees' daughter – another Bethan!

About this time I decided to leave London, and was fortunate enough to get a teaching post in Llanrwst, a town in the Conway Valley. I told Ryan of my intention, who appreciated that I was not quite built for cosmopolitan life. I felt more secure surrounded by hills. The years in London and my partnership with Ryan had been very fulfilling and happy. We had known thousands of laughs and no animosity. However, I felt that the time was ripe for me to return home. I packed my one and only suitcase and left.

At the Llandudno National Eisteddfod in 1963, the London Welsh were invited to perform John Gwilym Jones' commissioned play, 'The Story of a Welshman'. The play was based on the life of Morgan Llwyd, a famous 17th century Welsh puritan. Ryan was asked to play Morgan Llwyd. The play was a marathon. Here is a report on the production:

> For the first time in the history of the Eisteddfod, it became necessary to give a matinee performance for one of the plays arranged as part of the Drama week. The play was 'Hanes rhyw Gymro' ('the Story of a Welshman'), which the North Wales playwright John Gwilym Jones had been commissioned to write for the Eisteddfod, and the LWA Drama Group had been invited to perform as a mark of their contribution to Welsh Drama, having previously won the drama cup for the best performance for the last three years. And so Monday afternoon and evening, before two packed audiences of over a thousand each at the Grand Theatre, came the culmination of four months' preparation by the LWA Drama Group. It was a mammoth production with a cast of over thirty, and technical requirements were such that it required another fifteen LWA persons to undertake the work of production make-up and costume changing. The play took 3¼ hours and this perhaps was the chief criticism, for whilst the great leaders of Welsh Drama were loud in their praise for the production they felt that the play could have been shortened, and the author said after the performances, 'Any criticism made would be because of my fault, and certainly not the company's'. Raymond Edwards, Principal of the City of Cardiff College of Music and Drama, described the group as the best amateur company in Wales today. The performance of Ryan Davies, who played the leading role, deserves special mention for he was on the stage for practically the whole of the performance, and the extent of his remarkable gift as an actor was seen at its best. His part comprised of no less than one thousand lines and totalled in all some nine thousand words. He was well supported by the rest of the cast which, under the direction of Reginald Evans, gave two unique performances.
>
> *London Welshman*, September 1963

*Ryan.*

Ryan's performance was compared to that of Albert Finney who was at the time taking part in a similar play in the West End, 'Beckett'. Although I had left London, I was asked to play a small part, that of a tramp, in the production. It involved speaking two very funny monologues for comic relief, but for me it was a rather sad occasion since it was the last play I acted with Ryan.

However, I still appeared with him in the LWA 'Noson Lawen' which by this time had lost all traces of its farmhouse roots. In the Llandudno Eisteddfod we performed at the Odeon Cinema:

> The Noson Lawen at the Odeon Cinema on the Wednesday night again broke all records. The theatre held 1,900 and within fifteen minutes of the doors opening some 2,000 people had managed to gain admission. After closing the doors with several hundred still outside, G R Bentley turned to Rhys Griffiths, the LWA warden, and remarked, 'You have filled this hall to capacity and this is something that has never happened before in the history of this theatre'.
>
> *London Welshman*, September 1963

I still remember the opening sketch. As most people are aware, the main ceremony at our National Eisteddfod is the Chairing of the Bard. As mentioned earlier, the chair is awarded for an Ode written in the old Welsh metres. All entries are under a nom-de-plume. Nobody knows the identity of the poet, other than the Archdruid and a few officials, until the big moment arrives in the big pavilion. Everyone tries to find out by foul or fair means before the occasion, and there is more speculation as to the winner's identity than one would find before the Grand National! All things being well, the Archdruid calls out the winning poet's nom-de-plume, and the solitary Byronic figure stands up amongst the thousands in the audience. Our opening sketch on this particular evening poked a little fun at this ceremony. Gwenlyn Parry was the acting adjudicator speaking in strange Welsh, the like of which I have never heard before or since. I remember that I was acting the part of the Archdruid, wrapped up in a sheet borrowed from our hotel. The nom-de-plume of the winning poet was Eldorado. When I announced the name, the spotlight revealed Ryan standing in the aisle dressed as an usherette, with a tray of ice-cream tied around his neck. The audience exploded! When two of the cast, dressed as druids descended into the audience to escort him to the stage, Ryan started to run up and down the aisle, with the two druids in hot pursuit, trying to sell ice-cream to members of the audience at the same time.

Following the Eisteddfod in Llandudno, I returned to Llanrwst, Ryan to London. Naturally I did not have his company often after that time, although our friendship lasted just the same. From my understanding, he did not attend the London Welsh Association half as often. He was happier to be with his family; he was the President of the Croydon Welsh, continuing to perform for the West Wickham Opera Society as I have mentioned.

I saw him once during the year following the Llandudno National Eisteddfod. He came down from London to Borth, near Aberystwyth as a guest for the Welsh League of Youth. He had brought the The Three Taffs record with him, and played it endlessly in the basement of a hostel called Pantyfedwen. He was so delighted with the new sound on the record; his music was being backed by five instruments, and he became obsessed with the idea. For the rest of his life he was searching for a particular sound; whether he ever found it will remain a mystery. All the young people at Pantyfedwen were delighted. It was something new and full of vitality for them, a new experience in Welsh popular music.

He wrote to me occasionally. His letters were few and far between, but when one did arrive it was an Odyssey. He would write endless paragraphs about any subject under the sun that took his fancy at that moment – drama, music, film – very seriously. Then he'd get fed up with being serious, and would glue in a sailor's head that he had cut out of a Player's cigarette packet. A bubble would appear from the sailor's mouth in which he'd write some zany remark such as 'Ship ahoy', 'Bring the canoe into the house', or 'Hit the beaches'. Gwenlyn Parry had a letter from him that you could only read by holding it up to a mirror. Not only that, but the first sentence started in the middle of the page and the writing coiled out into the edges! No wonder that he enjoyed reading books by Spike Milligan, such as *Adolf Hitler: My Part in his Downfall* and *The Dustbin Milligan*.

He started doing a lot of television, and travelled down to do Welsh programmes for BBC Wales, TWW, or Teledu Cymru. Ieuan Davies, who had acted with him in some of the LWA plays, was as I have mentioned a director for Teledu Cymru, and Ryan did a comedy series for him.

When the National Eisteddfod came to Swansea in 1964, the LWA performed a play by a London Welsh playwright, Gwilym T Hughes. The play, 'Yr Aflonyddwr' ('The Agitator'), was based on the life of Socrates, described by the author as the most renowned beatnik the world has ever known. The play starts with Socrates taking his poison, which is conveyed in a mime. Ryan played the part of Socrates, and I remember the effectiveness of his performance in this first scene. It was Ryan's last amateur performance, and it is rather ironic that this occurred in Swansea's Grand Theatre, which was to become so important to him later as a professional actor. Mike Evans, Ryan's friend and personal manager gave me a few notes about the Grand's history which I am sure will be of interest:

> In 1897, when the theatre was built, Swansea was already served by one theatre and two music halls. The music hall [now the Albert Hall Cinema] was flourishing, the Swansea Empire [now called the Palace Theatre and regretfully a bingo hall] was packing in its audiences, and the Star Theatre in Wind Street [later called the Rialto Cinema and demolished in recent years] was a third very successful theatrical undertaking. The New Swansea Empire in Oxford Street was to be opened three years later.

The new theatre opened in Singleton Street was to be called the Grand, and it was to be just that. Lavish, luxurious and elegant with the latest and best theatrical equipment. A development for the theatre, which was not apparently welcomed, was the use of electricity to light the stage.

Now, over three quarters of a century later, the other theatres and music halls have sadly gone, but Swansea is still served by the Grand. It was in 1957 that a young actor was invited to the theatre for six weeks to put on six plays. Today, he is still at the theatre as Administrator – his name is John Chilvers. It was through his foresight and guidance that the Grand was to survive a period when theatres all over the country were closing their doors to the public. As a result of this contribution, he was honoured as a Member of the British Empire for his services to theatre.

The big debate in Wales at the time was the definition of a 'professional' and an 'amateur' actor. After considering many factors such as training, natural talent, devotion and experience the only logical definition of a professional actor is that he is a person who earns his livelihood through acting. Wales never had a theatrical history or tradition that is worth mentioning. Various people had made some efforts, with little effect up to that time. There were many heated arguments, and emotional dialogues spoken in those days, but no bricks were laid. I remember reading an article by that witty critic Gwyn Thomas in the magazine *Plays and Players* saying that Wales had no National Theatre, but as soon as two Welshmen met, the curtain went up! Famous Welsh actors such as the late Huw Griffith and Emlyn Williams found fame and renown in Stratford and the West End but they hardly ever set foot on Welsh stages. This absence of an English-language tradition in the Welsh theatre was even more lacking in the Welsh-language theatre. The Welsh language theatre was entirely based on the amateur, and Ryan was very much indebted to the amateur tradition, such as it was. His attitude towards his work had always been very professional, and work – mainly in entertainment – was coming from all directions. These demands, together with his work as a teacher, were becoming a strain upon him. He was like the man who jumped on his horse and rode off in all directions. He had to decide one way or another.

94

'The Women of the WI' – Myfanwy, Ronnie, Bryn and Ryan.

The last of the television series with their special guest, Ken Dodd.

*Stewart Jones kicks out the travelling minstrels, Ryan, Ronnie, Mari, Alun and Bryn.*

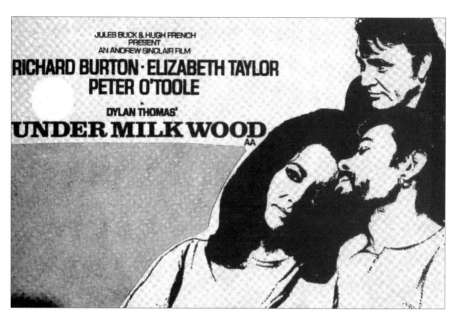

*With Richard Burton — "He is one of the very few really great film stars left."*
*hotograph: Raymond Daniel)*

*Ryan.*

*Summer 1972 saw Ryan and Ronnie appearing at the Central Pier, Blackpool in "The Good Old Days".*

*A serious moment during rehearsals for their first pantomime, 'Cinderella'.
The director was John Chilvers.*

*Two choruses of 'Sosban Fach' and then a quick drop goal into the circle.*

*Ryan accompanies on nose.*

*Audience participation with the Blue Danube Waltz orchestrated for Adam's's apple and nose.*

*Clifford Henry as dame leads the captain and his mate in a routine. Bryn Williams looks on in dismay.*

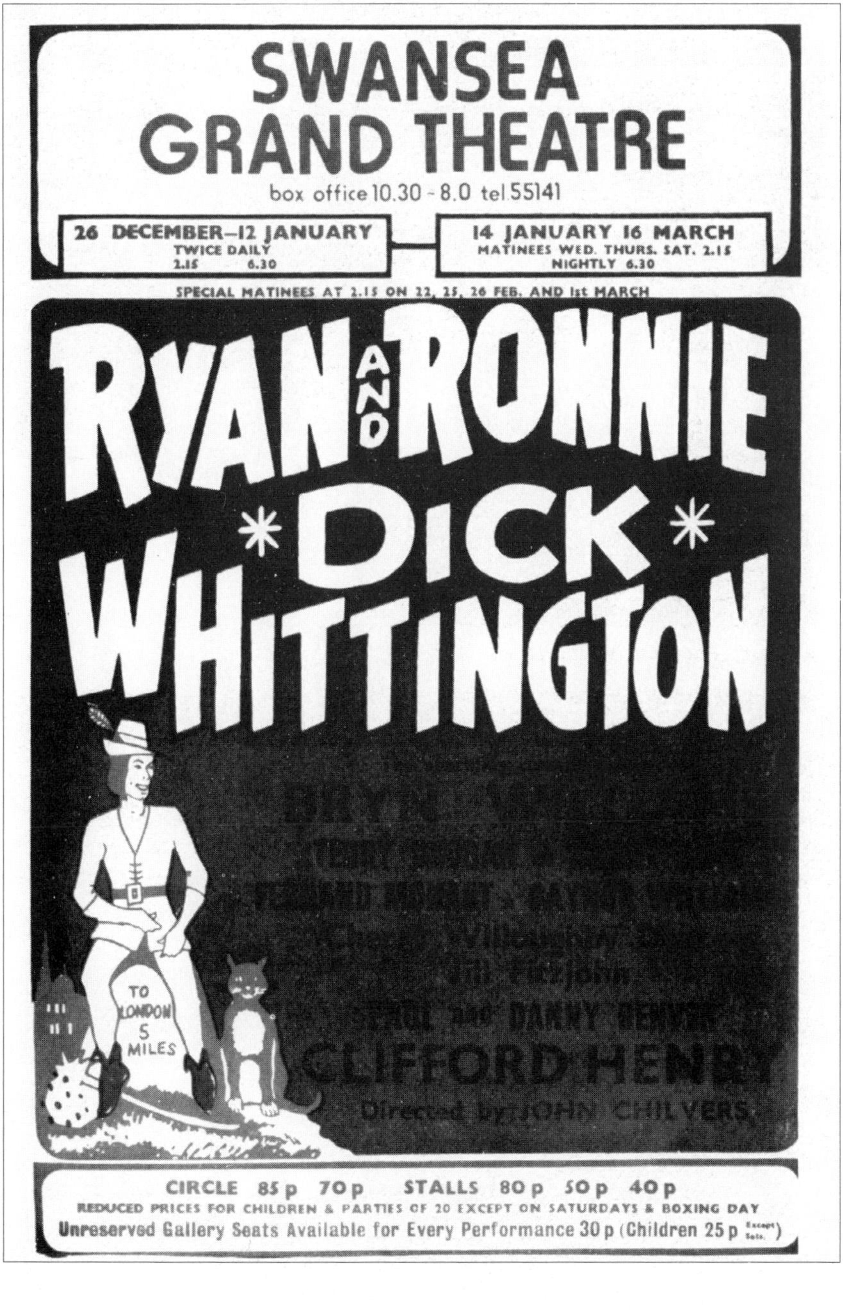

SWANSEA
GRAND THEATRE
box office 10.30 - 8.0 tel. 55141

| 26 DECEMBER—12 JANUARY | 14 JANUARY 16 MARCH |
|---|---|
| TWICE DAILY 2.15 6.30 | MATINEES WED. THURS. SAT. 2.15 NIGHTLY 6.30 |

SPECIAL MATINEES AT 2.15 ON 22, 25, 26 FEB. AND 1st MARCH

RYAN AND RONNIE
*DICK*
WHITTINGTON

BRYN ...

... GORDON ...

FERGUS MONKRET ... RAYMON ...

... Villains NEW ...

... Jill Fitzjohn ...

... BERYL and DANNY BENNER ...

CLIFFORD HENRY

Directed by JOHN CHILVERS

TO LONDON 5 MILES

CIRCLE 85p 70p   STALLS 80p 50p 40p
REDUCED PRICES FOR CHILDREN & PARTIES OF 20 EXCEPT ON SATURDAYS & BOXING DAY
Unreserved Gallery Seats Available for Every Performance 30p (Children 25p Except Sats.)

*Ryan.*

"Ron! Ron! It's stuck."

"Where did you get that from?"

"A big cow in Cockett."

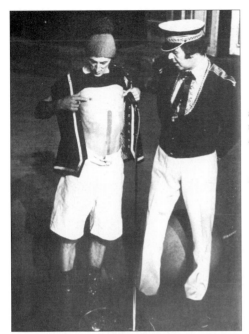

"I've got a fantastic job with the forestry now, and that, by there on my stomach, will grow into a coniferous tree or what is known as a Christmas tree."

"Don't be stupid! How can you know that?"

"I can tell by those baubles there."

*Mam, Wil and Nigel Wyn in the 'Our House' sketch featured in the pantomime.*

*Ryan.*

*Phyllis and Ronnie making final adjustments before another performance*

*Phyllis promoted to a traffic warden catches Ronnie out 'on a double yellow'.*

*"Then Wil and me won a competition and the prize was a holiday for two, at your own convenience. It was a bit cramped but we enjoyed it!"*

*A packed audience listens as Ryan and Ronnie sing their final song — 'Myfanwy'*

*"My boy, he's only that big. How old is he now, Ron?"*

*"32."*

*Ryan.*

*Ryan goes solo and reads of his new Welsh series in the* Radio Times *with Sheba looking on.*

*Ryan with his 'Golden Lion gladiators'.*

110

*Ceasar comes to Newport, Dyfed.*

*Ryan.*

*Filming in Newport, Dyfed. "I never fancied myself as a ballet dancer."*

*Playing dame, however, does have its confusing moments backstage.*

*The full company of Ryan's first solo pantomime performance – Mother Goose, 1974–1975.*

*Ryan.*

*"North Wales and South – behave yourselves!" (From 'Fo a Fe')*

*"Lloyd George is better than Stalin." A break in rehearsals with Mair Davies (producer's assistant), Jack Williams (producer/director), Gaynor Morgan Rees (Diana), Ryan (Twm Twm), Guto Roberts (Ephraim Hughes), and Clive Roberts (George).*

*Twm Twm converses with one of his pigeons.*

*Another scene from 'Fo a Fe'.*

*Ryan.*

*Ryan during the recording of his first L.P. – 'Ryan at the Rank', before
an audience of policemen!*

*The launch of his first L.P. at a Swansea department store.*

# SWANSEA THEATRE GRAND

Administrator:
John Chilvers MBE    Box Office 10.30 — 8.0 (except Sundays)    Telephone: 55141

| 26 DECEMBER — 3 JANUARY | 5 JANUARY — 13 MARCH |
|---|---|
| TWICE DAILY 2.15 and 6.30 | NIGHTLY 6.30<br>MATS . WED THUR SAT 2.15 |

ADDITIONAL HOLIDAY MATINEES AT 2.15 ON JAN 5; FEB 16, 17, 23, 24; MAR 1

## RYAN

in JACK & the BEANSTALK

**FREDDIE LEES**

GEOFFREY BRIGHTMAN    KAY COLMAN

**GOLDEN · BRANDY**    Jacqui, Tim & Wendy

CHERRY WILLOUGHBY DANCERS    BEN TABINER    BEVERLEY KAY

**JUNE and PAUL KIDD**

**BRYAN EVANS**

In association with
Howard & Wyndham

Directed by John Chilvers

CIRCLE 95p £1.15    STALLS 60p 75p £1.10

Reduced prices for children and parties of twenty except on Sats & Bank Holidays
UNRESERVED GALLERY SEATS 50p (children 30p) except on Sats & Bank Holidays

*Ryan at the harp, during a performance for a BBC Wales variety series.*

*Ryan with his musical director, Benny Litchfield, both 'on piano'.*

*4th July 1976 – Indepencdence Day for Ryan as he moves to Gower from Cardiff.*

*Relaxing at his new home with his children, Arwyn and Bethan.*

*A 30-1 outsider, joining in the fun at a Charity Donkey Derby in Mumbles.*

*Ryan.*

*A toast to the opening of a holiday home in the Gower for Spina Bifida sufferers.*

*Presenting an ambulance to the Swansea branch of the Multiple Sclerosis Society, following a fundraising Ryan concert organised by Swansea Round Table.*

*A break in rehearsals of the popular BBC2 programme 'Poems and Pints' – Max Boyce, Ryan, Mari Griffith, and Phil Madoc*

*His television appearance in 'The Merthyr Riots', together with Stan Stennett.*

*Freddie Lees previously appeared with Ryan in pantomime. They are
reunited in this production of 'The Sunshine Boys'.*

*The pursuit – Glyn Houston, Ryan, Roger Howlett as Dame,
and Ben Tabiner as the Sheriff of Nottingham.*

*Ryan performing at the last of his annual visits to Llanidloes – December 1976.*

*The little big man!*

*Ryan and his 'Rusty Steed' in his last pantomime at the Grand Theatre –
'Babes in the Wood'.*

*Ryan joining in the fun after a performance with a party of children from British Steel.*

*Ryan in a more pensive mood between shows. This was taken shortly before
he left for his holiday in America.*

# Ryan and Ronnie

THE MAIN FACTOR behind Ryan's decision to become a professional entertainer and actor was an invitation by BBC Wales to accept a full-time contract with Light Entertainment. The person who was largely responsible for this was Dr Meredydd Evans, who was Head of Light Entertainment. Merêd, as he is affectionately known by many Welsh people, has a doctorate in Philosophy, and had always been involved with Welsh entertainment since his student days at Bangor University. Ryan and I held him in very high esteem years before he signed Ryan's contract, and before I joined BBC Wales in his department as a PA (Production Assistant). He had become a national figure as a performer and composer for a very popular radio programme in the 50's, 'Noson Lawen'. He is one of the greatest exponents of Welsh folk singing and an authority in this field. In 1966 Ryan, Irene and Bethan left Croydon and set up home in St Fagan's Court, Cardiff, and I was delighted to have his company once more. Before he left, Peter Lloyd arranged a farewell party for Ryan in the London Welsh Centre. David Richards and myself were invited to London without Ryan knowing. He was onstage when we entered, and had quite a shock when we appeared. It was the nearest thing to taking part in the programme 'This is Your Life!' I have ever known.

The first series Ryan presented on BBC Wales was a Welsh music show called 'Hob y Deri Dando', which derives its title from a folk song of the same name. It was later recorded in English under the title 'The Singing Barn'. It was a series based around solo folk singers, and the programmes became very popular both in Welsh and English. Although he was under contract to the BBC he was free to do any other work outside television, and he was invited to take part in the Welsh Theatre

Company's production of Huw Lloyd Edward's play 'Pros Kairon'. It was his first theatre part as a professional actor. 'Pros Kairon' is Greek for 'a short time'. The play can be described as a morality play following the pattern of the classical Greek tragedies. It was a part that needed very sensitive acting – he was the little man being brought to his knees by the demands of a scientific, technical age. It is not relevant to Ryan's story to write about the establishing of the Welsh Theatre Company, but this was its second performance as a professional company, and Ryan was delighted that Wales was at last on the way to getting its own national theatre.

The foundations had been put down to some extent the previous year, 1965, at the Newtown National Eisteddfod. That year a very ambitious pageant had been produced by Adam's Wilbert Lloyd Roberts to mark the centenary of the Welsh colony in Patagonia. The story followed the lives of a young couple, from South Wales, who were with the first adventurers that went to seek a new life in that hostile land. The female lead was taken by Gaynor Morgan Rees and the male lead by a young actor from Cefneithin – Ronnie Williams. It was the last time I acted at our national festival, and the only time I acted with Ronnie. In retrospect it was rather ironic for me, having been Ryan's stage partner for years, to be acting with Ryan's future stage partner.

I remember two little stories about that production which tickled Ryan although he himself was not involved. In the third act, the Welsh voyagers had arrived in the alien land, and everyone had to do his chore, to get themselves settled in. To convey this industry, we were all miming to 'work' music in the background. Some were tilling, others sawing, some were hacking, others baking – everyone was miming some domestic or agricultural act or other. One character, Ifan Gruffydd, a farmer from Anglesey, a most loveable rustic character, was sowing enthusiastically up and down the stage. As he showered the stage with imaginary seed, I heard an old wag whisper under the sound of the music:

"Ifan, don't sow there, for goodness' sake – I haven't ploughed there yet!"

130

The wag that was miming the act of ploughing was being followed by his mate, who after three or four steps, would flick his other foot. When asked, "What the hell are you supposed to be doing?" he replied, "I'm flicking the horse's muck back into the furrow!"

I was supposed to be making a window for a cabin with ostrich feathers. I laughed so much – had there been a real cabin onstage, it would have collapsed on top of me!

Ryan did another series for BBC Wales, this time as outside broadcasts, called 'O Lan i Lan' ('From Village to Village'). He acted opposite one of the greatest actors in the Welsh language – Charles Williams (Non-Welsh speaking people may have seen him acting with Dame Flora Robson in my English version of 'Mr Lolipop MA'). The script was by Huw Lloyd Edwards, and Ryan played the part of the little man with the bowler hat, a character that he became very fond of. It was the first time he had acted in front of a television audience. When asked about audiences by Gillian Thomas, a student at the Welsh College of Music and Drama, Ryan said:

> As I am going on stage, I say to myself, 'They don't like you, Ryan Davies. Make them like you'. And this makes me work *very* hard at the beginning of the act. More often than not, thank goodness, I have come off having made them like me. Sometimes, they haven't liked me, and I want to run away somewhere and hide. I become depressed, and a pain to be with when this happens. I haven't made my audience laugh, and this, in my book, means I have failed at my job, and no one likes to admit failure. Audiences are of course essential to a comedian. You can do a play without an audience, you can sing a song without an audience, I film without an audience, but I'd shudder to do comedy without the reaction a live audience gives. This is why I insist that when doing TV comedy that there is an audience there that I can play to. They also spark off some ad lib comedy, which is marvellous.

Jack Williams decided to produce a series with Ryan under the title 'Igamogam', the nearest translation I can think of being 'Topsy-turvy'. Jack considered that Ryan's strongest assets as a comedian were his actions. Some of the sketches were with an elephant named Blodwen, a monkey, and a classic sketch with a deckchair. The latter followed in the tradition of Charlie Chaplin and Jacques Tati – the two masters that Ryan admired the most in the world of comedy.

May 1966 was the saddest month in Ryan's life; his beloved father died. He was buried in the Old Bethel cemetery, Glanaman at the foot of the Black Mountain. They had been very close all their lives, and Ryan was the light of his life. As Ryan's mother told me, "If he had to be rebuked, I was the one who had to do it. Ryan and his father never crossed swords in their lives".

When tragedy looms, there is a divine balance in life that helps us to retain our sanity. Ryan and Irene's second child was born on 14 June, 1967; a son whom they named Philip Arwyn. In the same letter that I have just quoted this is Ryan's answer when Gillian Thomas interviewed him:

> Have I any sadness that makes me a good comic? Good? Your words, not mine. I'm not quite sure what you mean by this question. If you mean, have I had experiences which have influenced me – sad experiences, that is – I would say no. I have had my share of sadness, losing dear ones and friends, seeing friends in trouble, seeing lots of people suffering, all these are sad experiences. At the same time, I do not, just because of these things, set out to say, 'Today I have had a sad experience and so I must be extra funny'. Is it a subconscious thing? Many of my colleagues are very sad people. Many of them haven't a care in the world. I am, however, a very serious-minded person. I worry about things which are important to me. My first concern is for my family. I have a wife and two children, who are my very dearest concern. Next I worry about my profession, atavistically. Comedy is a serious business. Some of my closest friends say that I am a sad little man. I do not feel

this, but do we see ourselves as others see us? I don't know. I have the ability to switch off when I come offstage, thank goodness. The onstage Ryan would be unbearable to live with offstage, believe me. Can you imagine being married to a 24-hour clown? Terrible. I am just a man who does a job of work, which happens to be to make people laugh. It's not easy, but nothing worth doing ever is.

Although Ryan's contract with the BBC was mainly to the Light Entertainment department, drama producers also required his services. He acted in a Chekhov play, 'The Marriage Proposal', translated by George P Owen – who also produced the play – from an English translation. Ryan played the part of Lomov, the rich landowner who visits Chubukov, another landowner (played by the late Ieuan Rhys Williams), with the intention of asking for the hand of Natasha (Myfanwy Talog) in marriage. But the offer ends in a wild argument about the ownership of a strip of land.

Another play in which Ryan appeared around this time was 'Y Drwmwr' ('The Drummer') by Islwyn Williams. It is a light-hearted comedy about a little man whose ambition is to play for the village band, but he is dominated by his domesticated wife, like a certain tropical spider, bullied by the female of the species. His big break comes when he is given the opportunity to become the band's drummer when the resident drummer gives up. He outshines himself in a rehearsal as a drummer, where previously he had only been the collector of the music copies. Only one obstacle stands between him and his lifelong ambition – the nagging wife. Having been given this great opportunity, his adrenalin flows and he gets enough courage to put his foot down, and the pigmy of a man becomes the king of his castle. This play was directed by John Hefin Evans who is now Head of Drama at BBC Wales. John told me about the scene where the 'worm turns':

When the moment came, Ryan did very little. He just sat down, and crossed his legs with an authoritive flick. He stared into Harriet Lewis' eyes (playing the wife), and the weakling had asserted his position. No dialogue was necessary.

It was the first time for BBC Wales to produce a play in the Welsh language with English subtitles. Aneirin Talfan Davies said:

> We get no end of letters from people who stress how they long to be able to follow BBC Wales programmes in Welsh. Various problems had to be solved in preparing the play, and experience will show how the technique can be further developed.
> If this first attempt goes some of the way to making a Welsh-language programme entertaining viewing to the ordinary person who is not conversant with the language, the experiment will have been justified.

There was also the possibility that BBC 2 might include similar plays in the same way that they used foreign language films at that time.

The system of subtitling had been borrowed from the BBC 2 method of dealing with programmes for the deaf, and was considered to be the best of its kind for television. BBC Wales can help solve the very serious problems that face the country by doing more than merely reflecting the community which it serves.

> The Corporation, in providing a public service of broadcasting in Wales, should avoid insulating the public from the realities of the world.
> We must concern ourselves with the turmoils, the excitements, the frustrations, the hopes, the fears of our fellow Welshmen and make sure Wales has its own distinctive voice on the air.
>
> The Western Mail, September 1968

The problem as stated by Aneirin Talfan has divided the Welsh people for a long time, and it is magnified when it comes to the terms of the mass media. The Welsh-speaking Welsh are in the minority in comparison with our fellow Welshmen, and the never-ending hours of English-language television tear the roots of our culture, and have a detrimental effect on the very existence of our language. The non-Welsh-speaking Welsh people and the English living in Wales seem to be annoyed that they are missing out on something when the few Welsh language programmes appear on their screens. It is a Catch 22 situation, and it would appear to me that this cauldron of animosity is only beginning to simmer. Ryan was very troubled by this conflict, and would have done anything – indeed he did more than anyone – to close this chasm.

Ronnie Williams, as I have mentioned, was born in Cefneithin, Carmarthenshire, or Dyfed as it is now known. His father, Iori Williams, had been a well-known entertainer in that area at one time in a two-man act known as 'Shoni ac Iori'. After leaving school, Ronnie went to work on the buses and as a reporter for a local paper before being accepted as a drama student at the Welsh College of Music and Drama in Cardiff. In 1964 he began working for BBC Wales as an announcer in the continuity department. An actor gets very bored with reading the news and announcing junction links between programmes, and Ronnie was asked to take part in a satirical series that Jack Williams had ventured upon, called 'Studio B'. Satire was the name of the game at that time. The fashion had been started by a group of Oxbridge students in a revue called 'Beyond the Fringe', and cascaded into television through the series 'That Was The Week That Was'. 'Studio B' became very popular with Welsh viewers, and two long-running series were transmitted. The Welsh Theatre Company decided to put on a review at the Bala National Eisteddfod in 1967. Somehow Ronnie, who had not appeared in 'Studio B', turned up and joined Ryan onstage to sing 'penillion' of all things! They sang a setting which Ryan and myself had sung on our first record. There was one major difference, the words were: 'The old town looked the same/ As I stepped down from the train…' – the words of the Tom Jones hit, 'The Green Green Grass of Home'. The reaction of the audience was such that they had three or four encores. Although it was on this occasion that they appeared together onstage, David Richards had produced a television programme in which they had acted. It was a programme called 'Ryan, Ronnie, Gill a Johnny', which also starred Gillian Thomas (who sings with the trio, Y Triban) and Johnny Tudor, the Cardiff-born cabaret artist and singer. It was on the strength of this programme, Meredydd Evans tells me, that he asked David Richards to produce the series 'Ryan a Ronnie'. Initially, there were two series in Welsh. Co-starring were Margaret Williams, the delightful and talented soprano from Anglesey; Bryn Williams, who had previously appeared with the Black and White Minstrels; Myfanwy Talog, and Derek Boote. Derek was a very close friend of Ryan and myself. He was a very good musician, singer and entertainer. In 1975, after a performance in a children's programme, he retired to his dressing room for a smoke, and a match fell into his costume and he was critically burnt. Ryan and myself went to visit him in the hospital in Chepstow – his strength and willpower, and the devoted attendance of his wife had kept him alive. We returned from hospital thinking that Derek had pulled through, but sadly he died a few days later. It was a very sad day for us, and the loss of this kind, professional artist was a tragedy Wales could ill afford.

Ryan and Ronnie wrote their own material for their series. This gave strength and weakness to their programmes. Understanding their own brand of humour was an asset to many of their sketches, but the pressure of creating half an hour of comedy every week puts a strain on one's creativity, and the material becomes forced. Some of their sketches were very memorable. The cowboy sketch which David filmed in a ruined lead mine near Aberystwyth is a classic. Ronnie was all in white – white cowboy hat, white six guns, white riding boots, white horse. He looked like Roy Rogers advertising a popular soap powder. Ryan, on the other hand, looked like Jack Palance in 'Shane' – everything about him was black, including his steed, or should I say bronco. David shot the approach of the 'goodie' and the 'baddie' with all the familiar clichéd cowboy shots

– through the legs, closeup of the holsters, closeup of the eyes, the music cut from 'goodie' tracks to 'baddie' tracks, and then, the climax. Ronnie said, in the rough voice of a toughie, "This town ain't big enough for both of us." Ryan, in an effeminate whisper said, "Pardon?" I nearly died laughing when I first saw that film sketch.

Another film sketch was shot at the well-known resort of Portmeirion. It was about two Spanish lovers courting. Ryan, as a nervous lover, serenades a beautiful contessa in the moonlight. After a few notes sung out of tune she reciprocates with a jug of cold water. Ronnie, the confident lover, shows Ryan how it should be done. He sings with his guitar and she responds with a beautiful smile. After being drenched three times, Ryan's face lights up when, on the fourth time, the cascade does not come. He looks up thinking he has won the heart of the beautiful contessa, only to find a toothless old hag on the balcony!

One more. The BBC scene department built a floating roof of a house and it was taken to a nearby lake. Floating on the lake, it appeared to be under water, with smoke coming from the chimney! The film then showed a lifeboat racing toward the house. As it approaches, a voice shouts from the boat, "Red Cross! Red Cross!" From below the roof, Ryan's voice is heard: "We've given!"

On 29 January, 1971, the press reported that Ryan had been offered a part in the film version of Dylan Thomas' 'Under Milk Wood' as the Second Voice, opposite Richard Burton who was to play First Voice. A press reporter in a column entitled 'Post Man's Diary' writes about Ryan's reaction:

> The lean, jester's face cracked in a wide Welsh grin as Ryan Davies spoke of his plum film part in 'Under Milk Wood': "It was a complete surprise to be chosen. It's very exciting and very flattering, but a little frightening. I never met Dylan, but I have been a great admirer of his poetry and plays for many years, and it is great to be given the chance to act in one, particularly with Richard Burton. I have never met him either. I auditioned for

the film, but you can imagine my surprise and delight when I was offered the part. It has given the Welsh scene a bit of a lift that they have chosen Welsh-speaking actors. It shows that they have confidence in us. I am looking forward to working with Richard Burton and studying his technique. He is one of the few great film stars left".

Ryan had always admired Richard Burton as one of the great actors of this century, but he came to admire him as a person during that filming. They spoke Welsh to one another, and they were both rugby fanatics, but more important to Ryan was the fact that Richard Burton did not try to override him. Richard treated him as an equal, and to Ryan, this was a sign of real greatness. He was very nervous when he met him off the train at Fishguard, Dyfed, but within a few minutes Richard Burton had taken him under his wing and his anxieties had vanished.

The film was directed by Adam's Andrew Sinclair, a Scottish former academic who had turned to the more lucrative life of film-making. He had been in love with the Dylanesque style of writing; indeed, his second novel, 'My Friend Judas', had been influenced by Dylan's writing. When asked by John Hall in the *Guardian*, 17 May, 1971, why he had tried to make a perfectly good radio play into a film, this was Sinclair's answer:

> Because I think one of the jobs of intelligent people is to make available to as many people as possible the best things which are written or known of. As a radio play it was condemned to a small minority audience. It doesn't work as a stage play or as television because you can't open it out in those media, but it does work as a film, where you can actually go on location to a wood or a village. I believe it is possible to appeal to the good taste of the British public as well as to its worst taste, although the British cinema spends all its time appealing to the worst taste. I also believe it is possible to make money by appealing to good taste.

In trying to put 'Milk Wood' on celluloid, he was faced with a characterisation of Voice One and Voice Two. In the radio play, they are just commentators; they do not assume flesh and blood like all the other characters in the play. To overcome this vital problem, he stole two characters from two other works by Dylan Thomas; 'Return Journey', and 'Just like little Dogs'. In 'Return Journey', Thomas returns to the Swansea of his youth to find himself. In the short story 'Just like little Dogs', from his book *Portrait of the Artist as a Young Dog*, he tells of two friends who return from the war to look for a girlfriend, Norma, whom they had shared.

In Sinclair's mind he had solved the problem of the Voices completely by doing this. He had half-solved the problem before:

> I had given the two Voices faces and characters – predominance to the powerful, brooding face and pale-piercing eyes of Richard Burton; foolery to the thin, playful melancholic skull's head of Ryan. Davies, the beloved clown of Welsh television, playing the jester to Burton's King, the imp to Lucifer.

The film ends with all the characters going in to the sea and turning into seals, led by Ryan riding a pig. Sinclair explains the action:

> If you study the text and go beyond the romanticism and into its roots, you will find quite another story. There's the theme of the walking dead, of the devil visiting a town, the theme of the sea and dreams, and the Celtic legends that seals are the drowned dead. All the dead come out of the sea and go back to the sea. There's a wild dream dance round the village pub (that's absolutely traditional) and they all dance out to sea and become seals; they have taken all their dreams back to the sea where they came from. All these things are in the text if you look for them. They are archetypal Celtic legends in base; my concern is to make a visual archetype available. Actually, I added one thing which ties the film up nicely. The devil rides a

pig in medieval legend and we have the Second Voice, Ryan
Davies, jump on a pig and ride it straight into cameras – it's a
hell of a shot.

The Guardian, 17 May, 1971

Sinclair, at the end of his preface to his screenplay of 'Under Milk Wood',
seems to be carried away with the mysticism of Welsh mythology:

> I sensed timeless powers of the Gwaun Valley, where the pagan
> stones still stand at the doorways and the mistletoe hangs from
> the wind-bent oaks, the powers of light and night, wind and
> water, stone and hill, crow and cromlech, Celtic cross and
> bleeding yew, which are still the old gods in that Pembrokeshire
> where the ancient Celts quarried stones to drag all the way to
> Stonehenge. And I knew that we only had to resign ourselves
> to the place and its doings to recapture the spell of Dylan's
> words and describe Milk waking Wood.
>
> If 'Under Milk Wood' works as a film, it will be because we
> were all the servants of the dead Dylan Thomas, who caught
> the essence of all Welsh sea-towns and made an incantation
> to them. We were not making the film. The film was the
> making of us.

I don't think it worked as a film, although it had some very good scenes
in it. I tend to agree with the critic, John Hall:

> While the prospect of an Eastman-coloured 'Under Milk
> Wood' is guaranteed to wring hosannas from the American
> Ladies' Literary Guild and sixth formers in first beards, I must
> admit it sounds to me like a sure-fire basis for a sloeblack, slow,
> black, crow-black, cockle-boat-bobbing nightmare. I used to
> borrow a record of the play from the library, and play it in the
> dark, and once when I was half asleep I heard it on the radio,
> which was where it was meant to be. To sit and watch
> somebody else's visuals for the established fantasy is to bid

farewell to one more certainty of youth. It is like coming face to face for the first time with a Co-op Santa who has succumbed to the embrace of caries.

*The Guardian*, 17 May, 1971

Rhiannon Howell, then my girlfriend, and I visited Ryan as he was completing the film. He was staying at the Fishguard Bay Hotel, and we had been invited to have tea with him. He was in his room when we arrived, and we were led to a balcony to wait for him. Before he joined us, the waiter brought a silver teapot on a silver tray out to us. Numerous thinly-sliced sandwiches, cut as though by a microtome, were arranged on a silver platter. I thought the Hollywood touch had gone to his head. However, when he arrived he picked up the silver teapot and started clowning, pouring the tea from an incredible altitude, as he had done in 'Charlie's Aunt' years before. "How about some high tea?" he remarked.

He had been to London to do some dubbing on the film, and had been invited to dinner with Richard Burton and Elizabeth Taylor. He had not met the distinguished lady before, as her part as Rosie Probert in 'Milk Wood' had only involved studio work. She arrived eventually, and floated into the room swishing a beautiful mink cape she had bought that day. Having been introduced, she gave Ryan a closer view of the cape, the fringe of which was adorned by the claws of those creatures whose skins had provided the material for this expensive garment. Then, to Ryan's amazement, she twirled it around to show that the cape was reversible; the other side was fashioned from the skins of little creatures even more expensive than mink – and their claws.

Some people predicted that Ryan's appearance in this film would put him on the international trail. It may have given him a lot of prestige and boosted his confidence as a film actor, but it did little to advance his career. It was rumoured that the film would be premiered in Wales. However, the celluloid version of Dylan Thomas' classic saw the light of day in Venice, of all places – with Italian subtitles!

While Ryan was in Pembrokeshire filming 'Under Milk Wood', he was also preparing an English version of 'Ryan and Ronnie' for St David's Day. This special programme, only transmitted on BBC Wales, was shown to Billy Cotton, Jnr., who was Head of Light Entertainment at the BBC. On the strength of this programme, they were offered a network series. Like the Welsh shows, the series was produced by David Richards, and I was invited up to London to the Television Theatre to see a programme being recorded. When I approached the theatre I saw the sign 'Ryan and Ronnie' in lights, and I couldn't help thinking of the days when we had tramped through the West End for five pounds. It had always been one of his secret ambitions to appear in the West End. Well, if Shepherd's Bush isn't quite in the West End, it's as near as dammit. The first programme was shown on BBC1 on 25 June, 1971. Before venturing on this project they were rather apprehensive about the whole thing.

> Welsh comedians Ryan Davies and Ronnie Williams stood in their bathing costumes on the edge of the Wales Empire Pool. But they are about to dip their toes in far deeper waters....
> In fact, the pair are jumping in at the deep end, to continue the metaphor, with their first English-language television series – to be screened nationally.
>
> Now the Welsh-speaking people of Wales have come to know and love the whacky antics of this talented duo – and the English speakers might have seen a marvellously funny BBC Wales 'special' they did some months back.
>
> But will they translate – and that's a good word to use – as comfortably into a full English series? Aren't they risking even their popularity in Welsh Wales by agreeing to the venture?
> As they waited for producer David Richards to declare that all was ready for the filming of one short scene in the Empire Pool in Cardiff yesterday they assured me of their confidence.
>
> 'It might not work, of course it might not work. But any artist takes the risk when he starts a new programme,' Ryan said. And Ronnie told me how they had been doing a series of

comedy concerts, in English, to sharpen their style, in its new language. 'It's true that at first we didn't get our timing as exact as when we speak Welsh, but now we have it spot on,' he said."

*South Wales Echo*, 11 May, 1971.

However, they need not have worried. This is a review of the programme:

AT LAST – a new comedy show to really enthuse about. For sandwiched between the Clangers and Marine Boy at the unlikely time of 4.55 p.m. BBC Wales have come up with their own bright mini Laugh-in which, if not particularly original in its concept, was presented with such style and professionalism that it put many a spectacular to shame.

Credit for the success of this production must largely be shared between its major participants, comedians Ryan Davies and Ronnie Williams. They can best be described as being akin to a Welsh counterpart to Morecambe and Wise. Not that their humour struck me as being particularly Celtic. Nor should it have been, for the best humour is international in its language. Regional influences just give it that extra bit of colour.

The format of the show ran true to the form we have come to expect these days – three or four studio sequences recorded on VTR, interspersed with several filmed blackouts. Some of these were very good and would not have been out of place in a Benny Hill show.

There was also a return to the domestic sketch in the Our House scene while the song and dance routine with the Boy Scout flavour was exceptionally well staged.

Others involved included a delightful singer in Margaret Williams while Myfanwy Talog and Bryn Williams provided sterling support in the sketches. However, the lion's share of the work went the way of Ryan and Ronnie who not only established themselves as a credible comedy double of the traditional school, but were also responsible for some very good material.

All in all, quite a turn-up for the book. As we are fast

approaching the peak season of repeats, producer David Richards should press for his series to be re-shown at a peak viewing time. If this was a fair example of his work it could more than hold its own.

James Tawler, *The Stage and Television Today,* 1 July, 1971

The sketch 'Our House' which appeared every week stands out in my mind. Ryan played the part of Mam, always at the head of the table, clutching a loaf, cutting bits of it for 'butties' with the mechanical action of a sawmill; Ronnie as the father Wil, a layabout with a convenient ailment; Bryn Williams as Nigel Wyn, the overgrown son who was besotted by his mother; whereas Phyllis Doris, the daughter, played by Myfanwy Talog, was regarded as a common hussy. Ronnie wrote the script and devised the long remembered line, "Don't call Wil on your father".

As in the article I have just quoted by James Tawler, they were often compared with Morecambe and Wise, but I tend to agree with the *Western Mail* critic when they appeared at the Grand Theatre in pantomime:

Ryan is a metaphor as much visual as verbal. And thanks to the Grand's intimate auditorium he has few problems with the translation from television or cabaret to the theatre.

While his comic personality dominates the stage visually-speaking, he has a fugitive quality that sometimes makes one wonder whether he is really with us. One might be tempted to talk in terms of Morecambe and Wise. The superficial structural similarity is there – the wit living off the fall guy. But there the resemblance ends. I find that their humour has a subtlety which is outside the sphere of the Morecambe and Wise comic operation. Ryan establishes himself, so to speak, on the retreat rather than coming forward.

While Ronnie's fall guy, if one does accept him as a fall guy, always has a dimension of compassion for his friend's idio-syncracies which Ernie Wise does not seem quite able to afford.

*Western Mail,* 13 January, 1973

Following their appearances on BBC Wales and BBC1, they were now household names throughout Wales, and were very much in demand. Not an evening went by without their appearing in cabaret somewhere in Wales. They were assisted by Alun Williams, Bryn Williams, Margaret Williams and Mari Griffith. Alun had a white Jaguar at the time, so Ronnie had to have one, and Ryan followed suit. They travelled gallantly through Wales like modern minstrels riding 3500 cc horses! This was the golden age of cabarets and concerts. The whole of society, both English-speaking and Welsh-speaking Wales, seemed to be fed up with watching television, and headed to village halls and concert halls to see their idols in person. Ryan travelled with Alun Williams most of the time. They had become very close friends over the years, and now Alun often appeared with them. To break the monotony of the endless travelling, Alun and Ryan devised a game of limericks. As they drove through the various towns and villages, each had to compose a limerick including the name of the town or village. I can't imagine the composition of the unfortunate one who first drove through such places as Bettws Bledrws or Llantwit! Ryan developed a keen interest in golf, and according to Alun he became quite proficient at this addictive sport, on a good day. On bad days his temperament would raise its ugly head – the ball would fly away, miles off target, often followed by the club and a barrage of abuse.

Since his boyhood days, Ryan had attended chapel regularly, and found fulfilment and peace of mind in his faith. One evening Alun and Ryan went to a service in Caernarfon before appearing in a concert that night. The preacher referred to Alun and Ryan, and in his sermon went on to preach about entertainment, saying that it was all emptiness, shallow and evil. Alun looked at Ryan. He said nothing, but Alun knew that he had been deeply disturbed by the minister's remarks; the self-righteous sermon had hurt to the quick. Ryan was a very religious man in his own way. I had always been conscious of this, but many people seem unable to understand that a clown can be a very serious person.

As soon as he comes off stage, a comedian will go to the dressing room or the theatre bar to relax. It is an enormous strain to be funny. As soon as he does this, inevitably, a member of his audience comes up to him, saying, "Have you heard this one?" I saw it happen to Ryan numerous times, even when he went shopping. Usually they are jokes one could never repeat in public. Alun Williams had found a standard reply. He would say that the BBC were most particular about copyright, and would not allow any material to be used other than from a commissioned source.

One evening Ryan, Ronnie and Alun were in the Rhondda Valley doing a gig, when the inevitable repeated itself. A local character came up to Alun and said. "Got the very joke for ew". Before he got any further, Alun came out with his standard answer, "It is a matter of copyright …" The answer nearly floored him: "Don't worry, mun, I'll copy it down for ew".

Through their reasonably successful television series and a new agent (who also handled such stars as Ken Dodd, Mike Yarwood and Vince Hill), Ryan and Ronnie were invited to appear at Blackpool Central Pier in a summer show called 'The Good Old Days'. Apparently, the show was a typical seaside frolic involving quick changes, dance routines and joke spots. A newspaper critic said, "I like Ryan. He is a highly talented and very funny person. I like the show too, because it does not rely on the double meaning joke and innuendo to raise a laugh". But he was referring to their own cabaret, not the Blackpool show. Reading between the lines, I detect that they lowered their standard of humour in the 'Good Old Days', possibly to appeal to a different audience. Robin Thornber writes about his visit to the Central Pier to have a chat with Ryan and Ronnie for the *Radio Times*:

> Ryan joins us and we talk about the discipline of doing a
> summer season twice nightly. There's the danger of becoming
> mechanical, relieved by throwing in ad-libbed lines which then
> get built into the show. In one spot Ryan had to come from the
> back of the auditorium, like a man who had wandered in
> looking for his dog. Ronnie had noticed that dogs weren't

allowed on the pier. "This is a pier," he threw in. "So's my dog," Ryan replied immediately. They kept that in.

Back in their dressing-room the loudspeaker relays the worthy chairman asking the audience if they have anything dangling. It sounds as if a lady is waving her underclothes in the air. "This is going to be a knickers audience", Ryan says, and it is. They howl at a wedding sketch where Ryan, as the bride, leaps from the stage and then clambers back up wearing red bloomers with an L-plate.

"This is why we're not sure it's us," Ronnie says later. "We like something a little more subtle than this." The dresser greys his hair for a Chelsea pensioner number. "If this photo gets into the *Radio Times*, my mother will be saying 'Get your hair cut!'"

I knew Ryan was not happy in Blackpool and wanted to return home to his family, although they had visited Blackpool for a short period. I also believe that during this period a rift started between the two comedians.

On the radio programme 'One Good Turn', Ryan was interviewed by Alun Williams, and asked for a record request. Ryan chose 'Man that is born of Woman' from Brahm's Requiem. "Here you are," said Alun, "in the candy-floss tinsel, the glittering lights of Blackpool, and this is your choice. It proves that you are really an old dyed-in-the-wool Welsh non-conformist." Ryan answered, "Alun, I suppose you are right".

Ryan and Ronnie returned to Wales to record another television series in Welsh, and then they added another string to their bow by accepting an invitation to appear for the first time in a pantomime at the Swansea Grand Theatre directed by John Chilvers.

Mike Evans, Ryan's friend and personal manager writes:

John Chilvers had built up over the years a fine tradition of panto-mime in Swansea. 'Cinderella' was planned for the following Christmas with Grand and Mars playing the Ugly Sisters and Ian Calvin as Prince Charming. Although Ryan and Ronnie had no previous experience of pantomime work, John felt that with their success on television and their local identity, their inclusion would be an obvious draw – but how could he place a comedy double act into the plot of Cinderella? He decided that Ryan and Ronnie would be top-of-the-bill as the Brokers Men, and, in effect, play down the role of Buttons. It was probably the first time that the Brokers Men have headed a cast in Cinderella, rather like the Cat playing the lead in Dick Whittington.

Ryan and Ronnie were overjoyed with the new venture. In their own words to 'Post Man's Diary' in the *Evening Post*:

> "I am really delirious about it," said Ronnie with sincerity. "I cannot believe that it has worked out so well."
>
> Ryan nodded. "If you had told me a year ago that Ryan and Ronnie would pack the Grand Theatre every day for three months, I would not have believed it. I do not know where the audiences come from, but they keep pouring in.
>
> "The strange thing is that I saw my first pantomime as a child at the old Swansea Empire, and it was 'Cinderella'. I still remember every detail of the production."

Certainly it did not include such routines as 800 children giving a rendering of Strauss's Blue Danube orchestrated for Adam's apple and nose, nor attempting to gain two points by kicking a rugby ball into the circle, which was included in Ryan and Ronnie's version. Cinderella proved such a success that the ten-week run originally planned was extended to twelve. Ryan and Ronnie were described in the *Western Mail* as being "local without being parochial, topical without disintegrating into a series of variety turns and, above all, [they] had a heart that understood children".

Although Ryan continued to do cabaret as one half of a duo, he also did quite a few solo appearances. He had put on a one-man-show at Cardiff's Casson Studio Theatre. Peter Davies, writing in an arts column, commented thus:

In his late-night show he demonstrates single-handedly such effortless versatility, one almost forgets to wonder that one has been accustomed to think of him as part of the two-man television act with Ronnie Williams."

*Western Mail*, 6 July, 1972

I remember going to the Casson with him, and during his hour-long solo stage appearance, all the characters I had seen him create appeared fresh before my very eyes: the harassed little man in the restaurant, the hussy traffic warden, the moody harpist, and the little man overwhelmed by trivial situations. Peter Davies writes about another item in the same show:

> Last night, in particular, some versions of 'Happy Birthday To You', rendered at the keyboard in the styles of half-a-dozen composers ranging from Mozart to William Mathias, were extremely subtle as well as being hilariously funny.
>
> *Western Mail*, 6 July, 1972

Ryan was invited to portray Adam's Saunders Lewis on the occasion of his eightieth birthday in a programme for HTV. The programme was called 'A Necessary Figure'. Saunders Lewis, born in Wallasey in October 1893, is regarded as one of the greatest Welshmen of the 20th century. The programme aimed to present a coherent impression of this remarkable Welshman to an English-speaking public. It interwove extracts from Saunders Lewis' plays, poetry and other writings – read by Ryan – with the conflicting main events of the scholar's life. The dramatisations showed how the public, political side of his activities related to the private, literary aspect of his character. I had discussed Saunders Lewis' literary work with Ryan since our college days, and he held him in very high regard. It was an important tribute to the great man's work, and the cast included such famous Welsh actors as Sian Phillips, Clifford Evans, Meredith Edwards and Philip Madoc. As it happened, Ryan and I had seen Sian Phillips and Philip Madoc in the original stage production of Saunders Lewis' 'Brad'

*Ryan.*

('Treason') at Ebbw Vale National Eisteddfod in 1958.

One could understand that he felt very apprehensive about such a part, not because of the acting, but because he feared that the public would misunderstand his contribution to the programme. Ryan said:

> This is a portrayal and not a take-off. After so many comic sketches in the 'Ryan and Ronnie' programmes, I'm afraid that some people might confuse the issues."
>
> *South Wales Echo*, 12 October 1977

He need not have worried. He gave a very sensitive performance and bore a remarkable likeness to the great writer.

Their television series in Welsh took a different format to the previous ones. They decided to make less use of television technique, using less film and stoppages in the programme. It was more like their cabaret programme where they had an audience 'in the round'. In one programme, Ronnie tried to conduct a serious interview with Gareth Edwards, the great Welsh rugby player, and Ryan came in and kept interrupting them. It turned out to be a very funny sketch.

Ryan continued to compose music. Most of the songs for the 'Ryan and Ronnie' series, both in Welsh and English, were his. Benny Litchfield, who was staff arranger for BBC Light Entertainment, arranged his music for the shows. Benny and his trio also backed the shows when they were on the road. Benny had been with Light Entertainment for many years, and had given Welsh light music a professional discipline which had been sorely lacking before. Benny formed a publishing company – Land of Song Music – and published some of Ryan's songs, such as 'Christmas? Maybe!', 'Ti a Dy Ddoniau' ('You And Your Charms'), and 'Blodwen and Mary from Abertillery'. They made a record featuring the latter song on one side and 'Myfanwy' on the other. They decided to promote their record. Where? Guess. And how? A press report tells us:

There will be high jinks in the streets of Abertillery tomorrow when Welsh comedians Ryan Davies and Ronnie Williams lark it up through the town.

With two local dolly birds in tow to add eye-catching appeal, the pair will be making a tour to attract attention to their new record, a single with 'Myfanwy' on one side – sung in Welsh – and a song called 'Blodwen and Mary from Abertillery' on the other. It is to represent the girls of the title that the two local lasses have been recruited.

'Blodwen and Mary' was written by Ryan Davies himself – and this brings into focus an ability of his which hasn't been talked about much until now.

He is an accomplished songwriter, and some of his creations have been performed by him and his partner on the programmes in their current Welsh-language BBC Wales series 'Ryan a Ronnie'. In addition, people like Margaret Williams, Iris Williams and Bryn Williams have sung his compositions.

He derived much enjoyment from composing music. Not only did he write the music, but also the lyrics. I rarely saw him during those years, although I did translate a few songs into Welsh for him, such as his song 'The Wheel', which is my favourite of all his compositions. In the same report that I have just quoted, Ryan writes:

> I find that songwriting is something I can fit in whenever I like, and it doesn't interfere with any of my other work. I have recorded some of my compositions, and it can be a very lucrative field if you strike it lucky. So I'll keep writing – you never know; some international artists might pick one of them one day.

Benny gave me a list of the songs he still has in the BBC Library – 'Della', 'The Little Canal', 'Let the Girls Sing' (Ryan's words, to Benny Litchfield's music ), 'When the Night is Long', 'Morning', 'Journey through the snow', 'Welcome to the Pantomime', 'La La La', 'Where were you', and some comical songs he wrote for the television series – 'Milk', 'The Police', 'The Butchers', 'Holiday in Switzerland', 'The Nation's Heroes', 'Tahiti', and 'The Folk Singers'. I understand that there is an intention to publish them all in one volume soon.

Ryan and Ronnie were asked to return to the Grand in Swansea to perform in the pantomime 'Dick Whittington'. It was during this time that Ryan met Michael David Evans, who became his assistant, his friend and later his business manager. Mike tells the story:

> Dick Whittington was out to break records – it had become the longest-running pantomime in Britain, as did subsequent pantomimes with Ryan. The other record broken was a world record – Paul and Danny Denver, as escapologists, were the speciality act and managed to set up this record by escaping from a straight jacket in the fastest time. Ryan thought this a terribly hard way of earning a living – 'and all because they are too lazy to learn a comic song'.

It was during this run that Ryan and Ronnie organised a charity soccer match one of the many charitable ventures in which Ryan became involved, with many football and television personalities, at St Helens Rugby Ground (!). In the event, Ryan was carried off after only ten minutes following an off-the-ball incident in which he ran into a goalpost. They had somehow procured a helicopter for the afternoon and managed to persuade Paul Denver to do his escapology routine suspended from this machine 350 feet above Swansea Bay on a bitterly cold Sunday afternoon in March. Yet another world record, and all in the name of charity. Ryan was invited to display his aerial abilities in the straight jacket, but he politely declined – "not for all the tea in Rhosllanerchrugog".

Even though the economic climate had resulted in the three-day week and petrol shortages at this time in 1974, it in no way affected the full-house signs which were shown for three months. With a second highly successful pantomime under their belts, it seemed certain that this comedy partnership would enjoy many more years at the Grand – but this was not to be.

On 4 May, 1974, a press relase announced that Ryan and Ronnie were splitting up. The papers printed headlines: 'Ryan and Ron Split', 'The Thin one goes it alone', 'Ryan and Ronnie bow out'.

At the time, they were presenting their cabaret show at the Double Diamond Club in Caerphilly. They decided to part because Ronnie was suffering from nervous exhaustion, and although Ryan categorically denies that there were any personal differences, their relationship had certainly lost the warmth of earlier years. In spite of his doctor's advice to give up work immediately, Ronnie insisted on working until the end of the week at the 'Double Diamond'. After their final song, the capacity audience would not let them go off. The two comedians, thoroughly professional to the last, did not let the occasion interfere with their performance. Ryan and Ronnie were given two standing ovations, and women pounced onstage to embrace and kiss them – it was their last performance together. To me it was a very sad, but memorable, occasion. Together with the thousands present, I had witnessed the final performance of the best double-act, to date, that Wales has ever known.

*This portrait, which hangs in the foyer of the Grand Theatre, reflects the great loss felt by not only his colleagues, but also his audience.*

*Drawn by the comedy actor, Clive Dunn, who appeared in 'Cinderella' at the Grand Theatre – December 1978.*

Ryan.

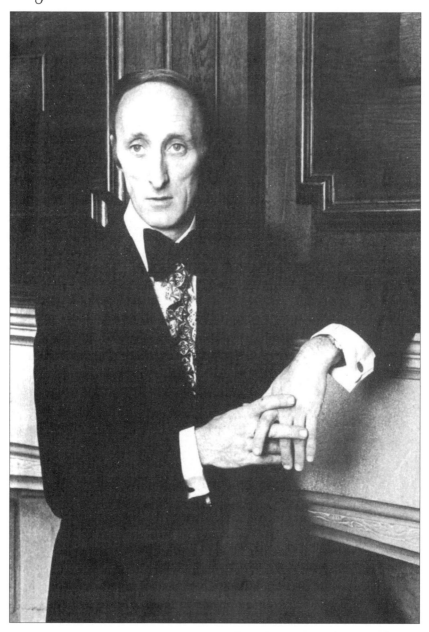

*Ryan.*

# A Solo Move

R YAN DECIDED to continue by himself. He had performed quite a
few solo shows, as mentioned earlier. Many people have
prophesised about how Ryan and Ronnie's career would have developed
together; others have proposed hypotheses about how they would have
developed had they never met. Theories hold no interest when it comes
to human beings. Alec McKinty writes:

> With all respect to Ronnie Williams – who was suffering from
> nervous exhaustion when the break came – I'd say Ryan, now
> that he has complete freedom inside his act, stands a better
> chance of the major breakthrough that his natural talent
> deserves than he ever has.
>
> Ryan himself admits, "I don't want to sound cruel, but I'm
> relieved I'm on my own," he said frankly. "We were both very
> limited as a patter act. Now I'm singing better songs, I'm
> performing better and I feel far happier.
>
> We had a responsibility towards each other on stage as a
> duo. I was wondering how he was going to perform, and he
> was thinking the same thing about me. It doubles the aggro, so
> to speak. Now I feel I'm able to develop and perform with
> more freedom."
>
> *South Wales Echo*, 26 October, 1974.

Alec McKinty continues his article, and Ryan tells him of his ambitions:

> Ryan puffed on menthol cigarettes as he told me how he was
> developing his act to appeal to an international audience. His
> ambition is sharp, and his two-year plan to hit the big time fills
> him with excitement and zeal.

"If I don't make it by then I'll have to think of something else to do – maybe directing films, or going back to teaching," he said. "I could do the clubs for the next 15 years, but unless they are the Double Diamonds, or, dare I say it, the Las Vegases of this world, I wouldn't want that."

Is there really a golden pot at the end of the rainbow? He performed his first pantomime in the Grand in 'Mother Goose'. He had always wanted to play a pantomime dame, and this time he was free to do so. Mike Evans writes about 'Mother Goose':

> In retrospect, Ryan met the challenge head-on and came through with flying colours. Perhaps his greatest difficulty was to try to relate 'Ryan' to the children being dressed in outrageous female costumes. The children had come to relate easily to him in previous years and they now had to accept him as Mother Goose. Although the audience felt that it did not affect his performance, Ryan conceded afterwards that 'although I loved every minute of playing Dame and was very happy to have done it, I doubt if I will ever play the role again'.

One of the highlights of any pantomime is the Children's Spot, and here Ryan came into his own. Six or eight children would be invited onstage and he would, for example, encourage them to play in his band. A selection of instruments would be handed out with the big bass drum saved for the smallest child! His teaching experience served him well for dealing with children; under these conditions anything could – and did – happen. Once the children were on stage, there seemed to be an immediate rapport, and they did what was asked of them; not because Ryan told them to do it, but because he had a way of making them want to do it. Of more importance, Ryan never talked down to them or ever tried to extract a cheap laugh at their expense.

The results of Ryan's band were always hilarious, with the children being the stars. Sometimes they were outrageous – Ryan recalled the four-year-old girl he had invited onstage, and he noticed that she was wearing a necklace with a little porcelain butterfly. Ryan stooped down and admired her prized possession, and asked who had given it to her. "Oh, John gave it to me when he was sleeping with me!" she replied. There was no answer to that.

Occasionally, the glare of the bright lights and the stares of 800 people got the better of some of the children. One or two would dissolve into tears; another manifested his nervousness in another way. The performance subsequently continued with the cast making constant detours around the spot.

When children became upset onstage, Ryan always insisted on seeing them in his dressing room after the performance, to make sure that their visit to the pantomime would not hold any bad memories for them. Ryan used to say, "Don't be worried – I'm a fella really".

Mike reports that the pantomime 'Mother Goose' was a great success. It certainly ran for a long time, but there are two sides to every coin. Graham Jones, a critic for the *Guardian* writes:

> According to the press officer at the Swansea Grand Theatre, last year's pantomime, with Ryan Davies and Ronnie Williams as stars was the second longest-running in the country (second to the London Palladium) and this year's, with Ryan alone (Ronnie has retired from showbiz to run a pub in North Wales) 'should be the longest running now that the Palladium has no panto – though Twiggy's Cinderella might compete'. He was always the best of the Ryan and Ronnie partnership and it was felt by some that he should have 'gone it alone' long ago. He is a tremendously versatile comedian, i.e. he can sing well, dance, tell a good story, give impressions and has shown his consider-able talents as a straight actor. He deserves international success. Yet, I wonder; I miss Ronnie. It seems to me that Ryan needs a partner, a butt for his humour. On a higher level, imagine Morecambe without Wise… Then again, in spite of his versatility, he is limited in range: his appeal as a comic is local,

and I doubt if it can be exported. Is he attempting to broaden his range as a comedian sufficiently, or is he expending his energies on his other talents?

He plays Mother Goose in a below-average production at Swansea this year. There is a high degree of cattiness about the affair: script, set, band, chorus girls, supporting artists. Ryan Davies deserved better. More than that, the vast audiences which pour in from the Swansea valleys day after day, month after month deserve better.

*The Guardian*, 9 January, 1975

For many years Ryan, during the time that he was with Ronnie, acted in a situation comedy in Welsh called 'Fo a Fe' written by my friend Gwenlyn Parry and I. Translated literally, 'Fo a Fe' means 'Him and Him', but 'fo' is the north Walian dialect for 'him' and 'fe' is south Walian for the same. A more realistic translation into English would be ''im and 'e'.

When I joined the BBC in 1965, I had written a script for a situation comedy in Welsh. My original situation was a young north Walian who had married a south Walian, and were living in a south Wales town like Caerphilly. The young wife's father comes to live with them, disturbing their matrimonial bliss. His name was to be Tom Thomas (Twm Twm), a collier who had never worked in his life, taking enormous interest in rugby, pigeons, communism and draught Bass. He was to get his son-in-law into all kinds of situations, and the young wife would be in a dilemma about whether to stick up for her father, or for her husband. I wrote the original script with Ryan in mind as Twm Twm. Meredydd Evans and Jack Williams liked the script, but they felt that it needed another 'tag'. I had shown the script to my friend Gwenlyn Parry who was, by now, living in Cardiff. Gwenlyn's father had retired from working in a quarry in North Wales and had come down to Cardiff to visit him. With my script in mind, Gwenlyn saw how excited his father was about living in an urban environment, and realised that he had hit upon the missing ingredient. The central plot would be based on the conflict between the

167

two fathers-in-law, rather than between the young husband and his father-in-law. We decided that the North Walian would be a person who had worked conscientiously every day of his life, was very religious, teetotal, and a keen supporter of Lloyd George; the exact opposite of Twm Twin, the layabout. Merêd and Jack thought this would work, and the pilot programme was recorded in Gosta Green, Birmingham. Four series of 'Fo a Fe' were shown. Jack had cast Ryan as Twm Twm; Gaynor Morgan Rees as his daughter, Diana; Clive Roberts as George, his son-in-law; and Guto Roberts as Ephraim, the North Walian puritan. The critics were very kind to us, and the public response very favourable. Even shops and boats were named after the series! Gwenlyn and I were amazed that so many non-Welsh speaking people watched 'Fo a Fe'. Ryan wanted to perform an English sketch at a show in Llanidloes. I wrote the following sketch for him; it may give a better understanding of the characters.

### FO A FE

*Set: living room with sofa, armchairs, television screen and radio. George comes into the room looking around, goes to other door – looks out – turns and shouts.*

*George* [Clive]: All clear – not a sausage in sight!
*(Enter Twm laden with beer cans. He is wearing a red and white scarf and a rosette)*
*Twm*: [Ryan] *(Singing)* Who'll win the triple triple crown,
Who'll win the triple triple crown,
Who'll win the triple triple crown,
But good old Sospan Fach.
*(Putting all the bottles on the table. George helping him)*
*Twm*:    George, my boy. First time in forty years. Having to sit at 'ome to watch an international.
*George*:  It's the debentures.

*Twm*: Bloody debauchery if you ask me. All those pliwtocrats from London – bought every seat in the Arms Park. All you want in rugby these days – a suede coat, shooting stick, and a blonde with big boobs. The spirit of the game's gone to the dogs.

*George*: It's not fair. It's never been so bad. Not one ticket on the black market even.

*Twm*: Never mind, boyo. First time I've been glad we 'ave a goggle box.

*George*: Do you think we've got a chance?

*Twm*: Chance! It's in the bag. With Barry John and Gareth – they'd beat the heavenly host.

*George*: The English forwards have improved. They've got a good pack.

*Twm*: Pack! Pack you say. That pack couldn't catch a rabbit in a butcher's shop window. As one old wag said the other day, "If they don't play better we'll have to cancel the fixture".

*George*: It won't be the same watching at home.

*Twm*: True. But we've got enough cocoa to make up for it. When those pliwtocrats are swigging their hip flasks – you and I will be swilling the old ale. "Cheers, old chappy."

*(Taking a swig from one of the bottles and passing it to George)*

*George*: Can't say that our front row is all that hot.

*Twm*: Never mind. The way Gareth throws that ball. Wow! Like a bullet. *(Picking up a small miniature rugby ball from the cabinet)* Remember that pass he gave Barry John last year? Wham! Went half a mile I bet. I'm sure he could find Barry in a coal mine.

*(Throws ball. George misses, breaking something)*

*George*: You couldn't. Diana will kill us.

*Twm*: You're allowed to make one mistake on International Day. She may be your wife and my daughter, but she can't bully me.

*George*: Want a bet?

*Twm*: Come, let's get this booze ready. Come on, Wales! Put the ball in! Get the jars. *(Going to drawer and getting a rattle out)* Must have atmosphere, see. If we can't get a ticket, we'll make this room as near to the stand as damn it. *(Turning rattle. Shouting)* Come on, Wales! This won't be a game, it will be a bloody massacre.

*(Turning rattle. Diana comes in carrying shopping bag)*

Diana: *(Shouts)* Daddy! *(He stops)* What's going on?

Twm: Nothing.

George: Yes, nothing.

Diana: What do you think you're doing?

Twm: Us?

George: Us?

Diana: Thought you'd gone to the match.

George: No tickets.

Twm: Not one.

George: No.

Diana: *(Seeing bottles)* What are these doing here, then?

Twm: These bottles?

Diana: What else.

George: International day …

Twm: We're watching the match.

Diana: Out! Out I say. Clear these bottles, every one. This minute. You're not having a beer orgy in this house. You think of nothing but boozing and rugby.

Twm: But Diana…

George: Listen, love.

Diana: Lovey-doving won't work either.

Twm: We've had some booze in the house before. You were tiddly as a bat yourself last year – last Christmas.

George: True.

Twm: Very true.

Diana: Last year Dada wasn't with us.

Twm: *(Getting angry)* I knew it. I knew it. That bloody north Walian git spoils everything I do. Can't understand why he didn't stay in his igloo.

*George*: Hold on, now, Twm Twm.

*Diana*: Call him father.

*Twm*: George, he may be your father, but since he's been with us, we might as well move to a monkery.

*George*: Monastery.

*Twm*: Or the Vatican. The pope and his monks live it up compared to us. They're hippies by the life I live. All we hear is hymns and chapel and Lloyd George's speeches. It's enough to drive anyone to crime.

*George*: Surely you can't stretch a point today, of all days. Wales playing England.

*Twm*: Yes. The Hindus have Ramadin. The Moslems go to Mecca. The Welsh have international day at the Arms Park.

*Diana*: If father came back what, would he think? Seeing all these bottles. He'd think we were alcoholics having a freak-out.

*Twm*: Rubbish. He'd probably have a tot.

*Diana*: Tot, indeed. He won't have sherry in his trifle let alone a tot. He's too decent.

*George*: Where is he, anyway?

*Diana*: Gone to St Fagans.

*Twm*: Typical.

*Diana*: He's interested in old things.

*Twm*: They should keep him. Put him on a stand and a glass cage round him.

*George*: He's OK. It's just that he's old-fashioned.

*Twm*: Antique.

*Diana*: Daddy! What time does the match start?

*George*: Ten minutes.

*Twm*: It's going to be a massacre. I tell you. Have a drink. *(Pours drink for them)*

*Diana*: Just one, then. *(Taking drink)*

*Twm*: *(Turning rattle)* Come on, Barry bach! Come on, Wales! Put the bloody ball in.

*Diana*: Daddy! Sht! *(He stops rattling)* Someone's coming. It's father.

*(Off stage we hear Ephraim singing a hymn, 'Guide me o thou great Jehovah')*

*Twm*: Dr Who's arrived.

*Diana*: Quickly, hide these bottles!

*George*. *(They go through a routine. Twm throwing bottles to George as if they were playing rugby)*

*Twm*: Hell, if they pass like this, England won't stand a cat's chance in hell.

*Diana*: Hurry up.

*George*: Catch! Coming through on the blind side.

*(Twm puts bottle down by his heel. Heels it and throws it on the sofa. They hide the last bottle as Ephraim enters)*

*George*: Hello, father.

*Ephraim*: Terrible weather. I walked all the way from Sain Ffagan.

*Twm*: Marathon.

*Diana*: Come and sit down. It's a long way.

*Twm*: Why didn't you catch a bus?

*Ephraim*: Exercise does you good. A mile a day keeps the doctor away. I've always enjoyed walking. Didn't expect to see you on a Saturday afternoon.

*George*: Couldn't get tickets.

*Twm*: For the match.

*Ephraim*: Match?

*George*: England-Wales match.

*Ephraim*: Supported Bangor City for many years.

*George*: Soccer that was.

*Twm*: Soccer! Dead loss – played by a lot of ninnies. Talking about soccer down by here is worse than apartheid in Alabama. North Wales

172

has given nothing to the national game.

*George*:   What about Dewi Debb then?

*Twm*:   Better for him to stick to news reading.

*George*:   Scored a great try once.

*Twm*:   Once. Barry John could score a dozen before the milkman comes.

*Ephraim*: I have very little to say to these sporting things. I find it difficult to understand how people can enjoy kicking a bag of wind around a field.

*George*:   You may change your mind.

*Ephraim*: *(Getting hold of transistor set)* I have a concert to listen to – Beethoven's Choral is on the Light Programme.

*Twm*:   Well, you go then.

*Diana*:   You should watch the match.

*George*:   You may catch on.

*Twm*: *(Miming to George about drinking)* Ephraim – it's not your cup of tea.

*Diana*:   He may enjoy it.

*George*: *(Seeing Twm's point)* You probably won't. It's a bit complicated.

*Ephraim*: Then I'll watch it. After all, it is Wales.

*Diana*:   Of course you must.

*(Twm and George look at one another in despair)*

*Twm*:   Switch on then. *(George goes to TV set)* I bet the boys are singing their hearts out at the moment. Pendyrus and Treorchy sinking brown ales like skittles. "Bread from Evanses, Bread from Evanses, Beer from the Royal Oak, Beer from..."

*Diana*:   Daddy!

*Twm*:   Remember France last year. Beat them at rugby and singing. All the old Frogs on one side singing, "A Frenchman went to the lavatory", and the boys from Cwmtwrch on the other "A'r gath wedi sgramo Johnny bach".

*Diana*: *(To Ephraim)* They sing a lot in these matches.

*Ephraim*: Some people sing hymns in all places but the right place.

*Twm*:  And the night in the Follies Bergére – with Fifi la Mere. She could swerve better than Barry John.

*George*: That's sacrilege.

*Twm*:  Doing the can-can, she was. *(Twm dances)* That's the only time that I have ever seen Sioni stop stuttering. His glasses steaming, his tongue sticking out – and this bird showing knickers and garters –

*Diana*:  Daddy! I am sure that Father finds little to amuse him.

*George*:  This thing won't work.

*Twm*:  *(Alarmed)* It must! *(Going up to the TV)* It can't let us down now. The only thing I watch on this thing is Tom and Jerry – and now of all times. *(Kicks it)* A crowd of thousands singing, and I can't hear a note.

*Diana*:  *(Going to switch)* I know what's happened – we've got a power cut. Yes, we have. What about the miners now?

*Twm*:  Serve them right. If they knew they'd lose the match they'd sail Ted Heath's yacht for him.

*Ephraim*: Who are Wales playing, did you say?

*Twm*:  They're playing ping-pong against Peking.

*George*:  England. What a crowd – singing away! First time we've missed a match.

*Twm*:  Too bloody true.

*Diana*:  Daddy!

*Ephraim*: I remember a big crowd singing in the big pavilion in Caernarvon. The day Lloyd George made his great speech.

*Twm*:  Here we go again.

*Ephraim*: I can see him now. His white hair glistening in the light.

*Twm*:  You'll be saying in a minute that he played for the Barbarians.

*Diana*:  Don't tease him.

*Twm*:  That's it. Wireless.

*(Going up to Ephraim, taking the wireless. Switching it on. We hear a*

174

*rugby commentary. They all gather round)*

*Twm:*    We're on their 25 line. Good boys. That's the place. Stay there.

*George:* Penalty – we've got a penalty.

*Diana:*  Who's taking it, did you say?

*Twm:*    Barry John. Over it goes, Barry bach – there's a boy. For your Uncle Twm – over it goes.

*George:* It's over.

*Twm:*    Ah!

*Ephraim:* Pity. Should have put it in the net.

*Twm:*    In the net! What d'you think they're doing; catching mackerel? Good lad, Barry, boy.

*(Further dialogue according to commentary Twm and George swigging booze behind Ephraim. Diana giving them glasses).*

*Twm:*    Now we've got them running. *(Atmospherics are heard on the radio)* Turn the knob man.

*(It gets worse)*

*Diana:*  Interference!

*George:* Continental!


## THE END


When one writes a situation comedy, after the characters have been established, they tend to write their own lines. That is, the writers know what the characters would say in a particular circumstance. Our problem was to find a new story week after week. More often than not, the best stories are inspired by incidents that happen in everyday life.

My father, a good fisherman, used to make fun of Ryan and I with our unsuccessful angling efforts. When I got home to our village one day from Cardiff, my father told me that he had seen two salmon in a pool not far from our house. I was ready to go immediately, but he persuaded me to have my tea while he put the rods together. I gobbled my tea like a starving chick and dashed towards the pool. As I came over the ridge my father was prancing up and down the bank like a man possessed, with a ten pound salmon splashing in the water. I lost sight of the pool for a few seconds as I ran to his assistance. However, by the time I got to him, the silver wet salmon lay dead on the bank, my father taking the hook out of his mouth. He told me that there was another salmon – an even bigger one – still in the pool. With avid enthusiasm, I started fishing, casting so often that the pool was full of foam! My father had left, and the other enormous, delicious salmon ignored my bait. Fortunately for me, a friend who worked in the slate quarry with my father was observing this saga and he came down to the pool. He told me to look behind the rock near the bank, and there I found a plastic bag full of salmon scales. My father had been given the salmon as a present! He had put a hook in its mouth and thrown it into the pool. He had waited until I appeared over the ridge and started his antics, pretending that he was landing the salmon there and then. His little prank had me fooled, but it turned out to my advantage. When I told Ryan and Gwenlyn the story, they thought of the situation comedy. Within a few weeks, we had written a television script where Twm Twm pretended to catch a salmon in the same way as my father had done.

Once again, it was time for Ryan to prepare for his next pantomime. That year it was 'Jack and the Beanstalk', and he was to appear with Freddie Lees, who later joined him in the New Theatre production of 'The Sunshine Boys'. However, Ryan became ill during rehearsals. I remember going to see him and I was frightened by his condition, but he wouldn't give in. John Chilvers writes:

> I considered postponing the opening, but Ryan would have none of it. I therefore had 48 hours to secure a stand-in. It was Gordon Peters, the comedian, who gave up his Christmas break and travelled down in order that the show could open on time. After a few days, it was clear that Ryan was still too unwell to return, but with Gordon already committed on New Year's

Eve, I had to engage another stand-in. Bill Kenwright of ITVs 'Coronation Street' came to our rescue, but because of train delays, he arrived just a quarter of an hour before the curtain rose. It was a matter of feeding him his lines as he came off stage, and this continued for the whole performance. But thanks to Gordon and Bill, we managed to pull through a most difficult period.

Mike Evans writes about Ryan's return to the Grand after his illness:

Ryan had been away from the pantomime for ten days and the audience had become accustomed to the pre-performance announcement: 'The part of Simple Simon will be played by Gordon Peters'. On the tenth night, no such announcement was made and the performance began with the audience unsure of whether Ryan had returned or not. Ten minutes into the performance and it was the lead up to Ryan's normal entry, the stage was clear and a figure stepped from the back of the set. The audience recognised the figure as he walked to the front of the stage and immediately a deafening cheer rang out and the applause began. Ryan stood there smiling as the applause went on... and on... and on. If Ryan had not raised his hand, I think they would still be cheering. It was both a moving and memorable moment for me, as it reflected the public's deep affection for Ryan.

*Ryan.*

# A Different Direction

RYAN HAD BECOME the most popular entertainer in Wales, as Trevor Fishlock writes:

> Ryan Davies keeps Wales in stitches. He is the only comedian in Britain who works in two languages and he is the only performer in Welsh language comedy who has achieved the rank of star.
>
> In Wales he has the kind of recognition that permits him to dispense with his surname on his billings and television shows. At 37 he is firmly established as an original and very funny entertainer, in Welsh and in English, on the stage, in television, radio and cabaret. With the ending of his long partnership with Ronnie Williams, his career is taking a new shape. Secure in his Welsh base, he wants to make his name nationally too. And that puts him in a dilemma.
>
> *The Times, 25 January 1975*

Trevor goes on to examine the development of Welsh entertainment and refers to its origin in the 'Noson Lawen' and the Eisteddfod as I have already explained. In the same article, Ryan shows that he had ambitions beyond the border. When asked by Trevor if he would like to appear in cabaret in England, this is Ryan's answer:

> Certainly I want national recognition. Like everyone in entertainment I have my ego and my show on the street. But I do not want to be sucked into a show business whirlpool. I want to keep one foot in Wales. It is my home and I want to contribute to the development of Welsh entertainment. I want

to keep my identity. I would hate to hear people say that Ryan Davies had gone English and deserted his own people. The problem is to fulfil my ambition and at the same time to hang on to my roots. I believe I can strike the balance.

Ryan continued to perform his cabaret acts in Wales, often supported by Alun Williams, Bryn Williams, Margaret Williams, Mari Griffith and the Benny Litchfield Trio. On one occasion, Margaret and Ryan were to appear at Treuddyn in Flintshire. The local committee had advertised the concert extensively with posters in many windows. Ryan arrived earlier than Margaret and was alarmed when he saw one of the posters. In enormous print, it read 'Ryan and Margaret Williams in Concert' and underneath a picture of Ryan with a chimpanzee. Ryan went around taking down as many notices as he could before Margaret arrived. Geraint and Margaret had been very close friends of Ryan's since our college days.

I had a letter from Mari Griffith telling me a delightful story of when they were in Llangefni recording a television programme. When actors are away from home, they seem to behave differently to ordinary human beings. Most of the actors that I know keep on acting when the curtain has gone down! On this occasion they were very bored, and after dinner, Ryan led the company into the lounge of the hotel for a sing-song:

> Seated at the piano, without a note of music in front of him, Ryan busked us through song after song after song until, unbelievably, we couldn't think of anything else to sing. Ryan suggested a bit of instant composition and produced the evening's dinner menu. After an impromptu piano overture, the hors d'ouvres became a dramatic recitative, the choice of soup the subject of a melancholy aria, the meat course received a thoroughly Wagnerian treatment, the fish was pure Puccini, the sweets were as 'dolce' as Rossini ever was and the whole thing climaxed in a coffee cadenza. Pure genius!

The television programme which he was recording in Llangefni was called
'Poems and Pints'. The original programme was produced by Geraint
Stanley Jones – now Head of Programmes – and it was later taken over by
Jack Williams. It was shown on BBC 2 and it gave Ryan his biggest
audience as a solo act.

In terms of television, he appeared in a feature drama produced by
Richard Lewis called 'How Green is My Father'. Richard himself explains
the thoughts and circumstances behind the programme:

> Most of us live in a valley of some sort, especially in Wales,
> but the Valleys in the plural and with a capital V have come
> to mean one group in particular, and more than a mere
> geographical definition. And like most places that everybody
> has heard of but which comparatively few people from the
> outside world ever visit, they have become something of a
> legend. Now legends may express an aspect of reality but
> they do not conform to it exactly, and if you confuse the
> one with the other you are in trouble. In strict social and
> economic terms, the long-established heavy-industrial
> communities of South East Wales have their own problems
> and their own character, and because they are living places,
> they have not stood still. They are not today what they were
> only ten years ago. Coal and steel, though still enormously
> important, are not the all-pervading presences they once
> were. The Welsh language is not as much in evidence as in
> former days, but it refuses to die, and the Valleys have
> thrown in their own aggressive brand of nationalism. The
> patterns of political power are changing, as are the subtler,
> less obvious patterns of social living, and of how people see
> themselves.
>
> 1974 was a year of stocktaking. Local initiative, never in
> short supply, proclaimed the Year of the Valleys. Conferences
> were held, committees set up, a thick scholarly book was
> published. It also seemed to call for TV coverage, but, in terms
> of anything likely to hold the viewers' interest, this was no

straightforward job. In fact, the more one studied it as a problem in communication, the more appalling it became. One way and another the whole subject seemed to have been done to death and there was nothing new to say.

Everybody by now is well aware that mining is hazardous, that miners are hardy and have been hard-done-by, that the boxers and footballers are world class and the choirs magnificent, that dalliance and beer are not looked at askance, that times have been bad and are getting slowly better. All cliches, by now a whole towering coal tip of them. So – and this was the decision that took a long time a-brewing – why not, as there was no escaping them whichever way you looked, stand them on their head? Mix the facts with the legends, the present day with the past; not as it was, but as it is remembered, the ordinary and mundane truth with the literature of sentimentality and nostalgia. And then let the viewers sort it out.

A poet perhaps was needed. Enter Harri Webb, satirist and balladeer with a wicked eye for the foibles of his fellow countrymen. He boggled and then grapples. Still it was no easy matter and 1974 was slipping by. Then came the catalytic cliche that precipitated all the others into some sort of coherence. In the Valleys everybody is related, everybody, as they say, is 'belonging'. Cross that with pedigree hunting and ancestor worship and you come up with an outsider who stumbles into a community where everybody is related to everybody else and to himself. An outsider who has read Richard Llewellyn and Dylan Thomas, and as a consequence has a not-entirely- accurate picture of what to expect. He has to be an American of course, a Graham Greene-type innocent abroad. There are plenty of these in real life, anyway. He has a series of traumatic encounters, but keeps his illusions undented. And if all the characters he meets bear a family resemblance to one another, then this provides an opportunity for a virtuoso feat of multiple impersonation on the scale of 'Kind Hearts and Coronets', always providing there is someone sufficiently versatile to carry it off. And of course there is Ryan Davies who can do just that.

*Ryan.*

The idea appealed to him, he sat in on the script conferences and came up with some weird elaborations of his own. And to comment on the ever-increasing perplexities of the main character, who better than Max Boyce, the most authentic voice of the Valleys in our generation. He worked on his own lyrics separately and sings them as a Puck-like spirit, who appears and disappears abruptly, but no more fantastic than the rest of what is going on.

The shooting of such a script was no mere matter of routine technicalities. Everything had to be done on location. The Valleys themselves became part of the action, the narrow horizons, the dramatic perspectives of steep stone-built streets, the odd juxtaposition of the old and the new. And the people of the Valleys played the role of themselves with tremendous relish. A whole streetful of housewives contribute to one scene, cheerfully aware that they were taking part in a big send-up of their traditional image, a renowned choir happily went into blackface and donned miners' helmets, caricaturing a caricature.

It took a long time to complete, and programme schedules being what they are, an extravaganza conceived for the year of the Valleys in 1974 will not now be shown until 1976. It thus becomes a timely bicentennial offering to our American friends, a typical tongue-in-cheek Valleys legpull which carries its own warning to any of them who may be tempted to unearth their Welsh ancestors. There is no knowing what they may find.

Ryan acted so many characters in 'How Green was My Father', and I believe that it was the best thing he ever did on television excepting two other programmes, 'Welsh Not' and 'The Merthyr Riots'. A critic for the *South Wales Evening Post* writes about 'How Green was My Father':

Ryan Davies played too many parts to count in 'How Green Was My Father', a tongue-in-cheek look at contemporary Wales which was refreshingly satirical. Away went the

182

traditional outlook. The pit-head made a brief appearance, but the American visitor searching for his past (played by Ryan) saw it off with a 'Gee, how picturesque can you get? Now I feel at home'.

This non-sentimental, almost sacrilegious view of Wales by writer Harri Webb dealt a hammer blow to the idea that Wales is a parochial cleft stick. Arsenal was sprayed over the station wall and not Abertillery.

There was a deliberate debt to Hollywood. The American stepped off the diesel train at Jenkinstown just like Gary Cooper did in 'High Noon' and the parody was complete when he stood in the graveyard of Jerusalem Chapel with rain streaking down his face at the end of the film.

Dylan Thomas did not go untapped. Jerusalem's minister, randy in this case and again played by Ryan, was Eli Jenkins from 'Under Milk Wood', and Harri Webb deliberately paraphrased Thomas's 'Fern Hill' in the graveyard scene.

The whole thing was brilliantly written, produced and performed and Ryan emerged as a truly superb character actor. He surely is poised to leap out of his Welsh straight jacket.

'Welsh Not' and 'The Merthyr Riots' were drama-documentaries, produced by Merfyn Williams and directed by Brydan Griffiths. There is one final scene in 'The Merthyr Riots' where Ryan enters as the little man who comes to polish the oak table and the chairman's chair in the Council chamber. The little man is not funny any more, his few words tell of the frustration of ordinary people being thwarted by bureaucracy. In my opinion, this was Ryan at his best once again – he had changed the masks completely; the mask of tears had taken over from the mask of laughter.

This trait in Ryan's career had also occurred in his theatre work when he appeared in the New Theatre, Cardiff in Neil Simon's American comedy 'The Sunshine Boys'. He played the part of Willie Clarke with Bill Owen, of television's 'Last of the Summer Wine', playing the part of

Al Lewis. Clarke and Lewis were, at one time, so the story goes, just about the greatest vaudeville team in the whole of the United States, but eleven years ago Lewis walked out and Clarke never forgave him. That is the background to the story, which takes as its starting point the suggestion that the two should team up again to make a television programme about the history of comedy. It was a theme that Ryan was familiar with in his own career.

> "I think Willie Clarke is a part I could do really well," he told me. "I'm so keenly interested in doing this and I want it to happen. Perhaps if I make a success of an elderly American-Jew, people will say, 'Well, at least he can get out of that Welsh thing'. And I want Welsh people to say that too."
> Chris Stuart, *The Western Mail,* 18 October 1976

When I saw the production I did not think that it came off, basically because the timing was wrong, except ironically in the scene in the television studios, which I thought was excellent. Whereas he had, years previously, found it difficult to change from theatre acting to television, the reverse occurred this time, when he came to the theatre to do 'straight' acting. I believe that Ryan had hoped that 'The Sunshine Boys' would have put him on a bigger map, theatrically, but sadly for him, it did not happen.

In a radio interview with T Glynne Davies, Jack Williams had this to say:

*T G D*: Ronnie had said that acting was Ryan's greatest gift. Jack?
*J W*: I would tend to agree. Everyone has talked about the many talents that Ryan had. In a way, that very fact, that he was so versatile, hindered his development. He did not concentrate on any one specific talent. By now, however, I believe that he had reached a climax in his professional career where he was more selective about the work he accepted. He was going to concentrate on his acting ability which, as I said, was his strongest gift.

By this time, Ryan was performing in English more than at any other time in his career, but he still did a lot of work in the Welsh language. He did a programme for me in a series that I was asked to produce. (Throughout the years with the BBC, I had not worked with him apart from scripting 'Fo a Fe', which Jack produced.) The series was called 'Ar Ei Ben Ei Hun' ('On his own'). Not that the one programme he did for me in this series needed much production; it was a one-man show in front of cameras. However, Jack asked me to produce a series in Welsh called 'Ryan' and it was a thrilling moment for me when a reporter friend of ours from our college days, Arthur Williams, wrote in his column in the *Daily Post*, 'Two pals get back together'.

I wanted to show his versatility as an entertainer and as an actor. I decided that the show should have an audience, like the last series of 'Ryan and Ronnie'. I invited guest artists, Anne Griffiths, Delme Bryn Jones, a folk dancing group, Margaret Williams, the Richard Williams Male Voice Choir and others. Although these artists performed their own speciality act by themselves, Ryan would join them for a second item. He played a harp duet with Anne, he sang a duet with Delme, and danced with the folk dancers. The item he performed with Richard Williams' choir was particularly memorable. They sang the well-known Russian folk song 'Kalinka', and when the tenor solo came, Ryan appeared in the back row dressed as a Cossack, pushing his way through the Choir singing a high note. He was brilliant, and the choristers could barely stop laughing. I wanted to show his ability to project visual comedy as well, so film effort was essential.

Since the time of 'Under Milk Wood', Ryan had a deep affection for north Pembrokeshire and the people of that area. Since he wrote all his own material, he had the kind of locations which North Pembrokeshire had to offer. I went down with my Production Assistant at the time, Iwan Griffiths, to 'recce' the locations. Purely by chance, we found the Golden Lion in Trefdraeth (Newport, Pembrokeshire). At a later date, my third honour was bestowed on me by Glyn and Penny Rees of the Lion when I became godfather for the third time to their little girl – Bethan. Ryan took a photograph, which is my most treasured possession, of my three god-children, his own daughter Bethan, David's daughter Bethan, and Glyn's daughter Bethan with myself. Glyn helped me find the locations that I was looking for and also found extras for my filming from amongst the local people.

In one film insert, Ryan reached the shores of Newport, dressed as Julius Caesar. He was rowed by four members of the Golden Lion's rowing team! Heaven knows what would have happened to them had they been extras in the Roman galleon rowing scene in Ben Hur! After the fourth take, they managed to get the boat in the right camera position and Ryan waded ashore to say the immortal lines:

"Veni, Vidi…"

He forgets and says;

"Oh hell, I'll come back next week."

In another film insert, Ryan was dressed as Phyllis driving the local bus. He picks up various rural passengers on the route, including a lady with a nanny-goat. Molly Litchfield was our wardrobe supervisor on the filming, and she naturally dressed the local lady in an old mac and dirty wellingtons. However, the extra returned after lunch-break dressed in her Sunday best, and when Molly asked why she had changed into her own clothes, she said, "Can't go on telly dressed like that!"

I shot another film insert by a local lake. It was a sketch about a Welsh Hiawatha. What happened next was a nightmare to any film director on a low budget – it rained cats and dogs, it was cold, and aircraft pilots decided to fly overhead between showers, somewhat inappropriately for an Indian reservation. Ryan had to row a canoe, and as he approached the shore it became evident that his legs went through the bottom of the canoe and that it was only strapped to his body with a pair of braces. Any actor who had to face the incredibly cold water the fourth time could have objected, despite having a wet-suit under his Indian 'drag'. Not Ryan; he would not give in – ever. In the end, although I was desperate to get the film in the can, I had to say that enough was enough. He would never say it himself.

He had established his own recording company – Black Mountain Records, operated by Mike Evans. The first major venture was the recording of the LP 'Ryan at the Rank' at the Top Rank in Swansea. There were twelve musicians in the pit and the music was arranged by Benny Litchfield, with BBC Wales' Des Bennett as sound engineer. If you listen to this LP and its follow-up, I am sure you will enjoy it as much as the Swansea audience did.

Ryan and the family had moved to Swansea by this time. He expressed his feelings on his first LP – 'Swansea, it's my kind of town, Swansea is...'

In 1977, Ryan appeared in his fifth pantomime at the Grand Theatre, 'Babes in the Wood', playing the part of the Good Robber opposite Glyn Houston who played the Bad Robber. Glyn Houston, in my opinion, is one of Wales' best actors, but more than this, he is a very kind and warm person. It was the first time he had appeared in pantomime, and Ryan told me that he enjoyed acting with Glyn Houston more than anyone he had been on stage with.

I went to a performance with Gwenlyn, and discussed a new series of 'Fo a Fe'. Ryan's daughter, Bethan, was acting as his dresser. We were discussing the series with him in the dressing room, as the tannoy transmitted the performance from the stage. Suddenly, Ryan would vanish to perform his bit, then he'd return to the dressing room, to pick up the conversation while Bethan helped him into his next costume. This went on quite a few times during the pantomime. Gwenlyn and myself were quite amazed – returning home to Cardiff we thought we had a new theme for another situation comedy!

Mike Evans writes about another aspect of Ryan's life during this time:

As many charitable organisations in Wales will bear out, Ryan could never say 'no' to giving them some form of assistance. This took the form of opening fetes, riding in Donkey Derbies, appearing in concerts, compering 'It's a Knockout' competitions or simply visiting patients in special homes or hospitals. One fond memory remains with me. Ryan was in rehearsals for his last pantomime and one evening attended a charity concert at a Swansea club for two soldiers who had been badly injured while serving in Northern Ireland and lay seriously ill in hospital. Members of their families were present and even though Christmas was fast approaching, the evening was filled with obvious sadness over the plight of these two young Swansea men and Christmas was furthest from everybody's thoughts. Without any announcement, Ryan stood alone on the stage and started to sing: 'I'm dreaming of a White Christmas, just like the ones we used to know...' A few voices started to join in from the audience and soon all those present were singing. I had never before, or since, heard Ryan sing *that* song but it expressed what he felt and with respect to Bing Crosby, I have never heard it sung with such depth and emotion as on that evening.

Ryan did an enormous amount for charity, for the blind, the deaf, for the mentally handicapped; he just could not say 'no'.

Recently Mike showed me an article Ryan had written for the *Western Mail*. I have been given the original script by Irene in Ryan's own writing, and I shall always treasure it. To me, it epitomises everything. These are Ryan's words on the subject of humour in Wales:

> Did you hear the one about Dai and Will going to the International at Twickenham? Well, that night Dai and Will went down to Soho, and...
>
> It could be the beginning of any one of a hundred gags – though in Wales we prefer to call them stories – that you have

heard so many times before. Where would we be without Dai and Will? They have been to Twickenham together ever since we allowed the English the fixture; they have attended every National Eisteddfod ever since Hywel Dda realised he was onto a good thing; they went over the top together at the Somme and Vimy Ridge and plucked the Zulu's feather at Rourke's Drift, and still they go marching on. 'Aye, well, they're part of Welsh Humour, see'.

Welsh Humour. Now there's a phrase for you. There's one for all the pundits to conjure with. Can't you just see them, in the bars and pubs, in the cottages and the mansions, discussing and thrashing our important issues on Welsh Humour? Pretty soon now, our educationists will have it included in the 'O' level syllabus. There will be another three R's for us to worry our children with. Religion, Rugby and Rollick, without which conversation in Wales would be limited to the weather and... Well, there you are. And who knows, one day, the students in our universities will be allowed to read 'Welsh Humour', and graduation day will be an even bigger laugh. 'Gaudeamus Igitur' will be replaced by a rousing chorus of 'I Wanna Be Happy' and they will walk to the podium in a yellow gown with a purple tie which lights up, and receive their scrolls. B.A. Dip. Hum (Aber.). The board of examiners would consist of the entire panel of 'New Faces', ych-a-fi, who would then be sentenced to a never-ending Summer Season at the Palladium, Rhos-y-bol (Oh yes, it does exist. It's in Anglesey. Maybe I lied about the Palladium – it's the Colliseum.).

But hold on, dear readers. This humour business is a serious business. So serious, in fact, that there is to be a symposium on humour in Cardiff soon. It's a fact. A number of eminent psychologists and psychiatrists are getting together to find out what makes the nation laugh, and this couch of psychiatrists, or whatever the collective term is for them – perhaps suite of psychiatrists would be suitable – anyway all of these eminent men are to be addressed by none other than Prof. Ken Dodd from the Department of Giggleology, University of Knotty Ash. Now whether you agree with this kind of laugh-in is neither here not there. Personally, I've got about as much interest in it as I have in the effect of the Gulf Stream on the mating habits of a Peruvian Yak. I suppose being a professional comic, I should try to find out what makes us laugh, but I'm one of those people who say and do something which I think is funny; and thankfully, my audience laugh, bless them.

My type of humour is, of course, Welsh, and that poses the sixty-four thousand dollar question – what is Welsh Humour? Where do we find it? Does it in fact exist?

Surely we do not have exclusive rights on the Dai and Will situation. I'm sure there must be a Russian comic somewhere at this moment telling the story about Yuri and Ivan going to see the Dynamos, and finding themselves in the Red district, if you'll pardon the pun.

"But Yuri knew what she wanted, aye."

"His photo of Barrislov Johnsky."

This must surely be true of them also. So what is Welsh Humour? I'm not completely sure that I know what it is. I can tell what it is not. It is not the slick, so-called sophisticated humour that some Americans throw at us on our TV screens. Neither is it that infantile giggly rubbish that Donny and Marie Osmond give us, oh-so-thinly disguised as comedy.

I don't think we go for the satirical humour of some English comics either, and most certainly not for the blue stand-up comic. So what do we go for? If we have to define it, and I think it's a shame that we do, I would say that the humour of Wales is to do with her people, with her 'characters'. 'He's a character, aye', and 'Duw, he's a card when he gets going' are phrases we have all heard many times, and it is an extension of the 'characters' and 'cards' which make us Welsh laugh. Remember Mam and Wil? There are thousands of them up and down the country, our versions were only slightly larger than life... or were they? And we laughed at them, indeed at ourselves.

I was once told by a comic that the Welsh cannot laugh at themselves, and that he had proved *that* theory time and time again. His big problem is that he is English, and his 'Look you, indeed to goodness' quips were going down with his audiences like lead balloons. Oh yes, we'll laugh at ourselves alright, as long as it's us who's doing the ribbing. Mind you, I was once accused of taking the micky out of the Welsh. I ask you. Me, who was weaned on laverbread and Welsh cakes – together. Well, if I, and my Welsh colleagues can't do it, who can?

Whereas I am not entirely convinced that there is such a thing as Welsh Humour, I am convinced there are traits of humour which belong exclusively to us, one of them being our insistence on giving everyone nicknames. In this, we resemble the Red Indians, who called their warriors Running Bear, Crazy Horse or Swift Arrow, although I must admit that Evans the Death, Bessie the Milk and Dai Bread do sound a little less lyrical than Shining Water and Little Red Deer of the Forest.

The practice of naming a son or daughter after the parent is a commonplace one and a very old one. Sion *ap* Sion means John the son of John. Dafydd ap Dafydd is a perfectly respectable, aye, e'en honourable name. Dai ap Dai smacks a little of disrespect, while Dai Dai, which means exactly the same, is very basic indeed. Occupations also provide us with fodder for nicknames. I once met a chemist who was known as Wil Pilsen (Will the Pill), though I suspect that in this permissive age, this would be more apt for the head of a Family Planning Clinic.

Sir David Maxwell Fyffe, when he was Secretary for Wales, was known as Dai Bananas, for obvious reasons. Her Royal Highness Princess Margaret on her marriage to Lord Snowden, who had family connections in Bontnewydd Gwynedd, was known as Maggie Bont. We respect no one. I suppose the cleverest one of all was the name given to the man who had but one tooth in the middle-top of his mouth – he was promptly named Dai Central Eating. A classic one, that. And no doubt

*Ryan.*

you have your favourite, and each town and village boasts of many such affectionate nicknames. The strange and wonderful thing is although they sound insulting, mocking and often downright cruel, there is no malice in them at all. There are many who believe that humour should be barbed and cutting – and no doubt such humour has its place – but Welsh Humour is never cruel. Sometimes uncomfortable, yes, but never cruel.

I cannot hope to cover all those aspects of our varied society which provide us with a laugh or two. You have your own views on this. You could argue that the Humour of Wales is to be found in the mines of the Rhondda, in the slate quarries of Gwynedd, in the farming communities of Powys and Dyfed, in the industrial parts of Glamorgan and Clwyd, in the chapels, on the rugby fields, in the choirs and in the schools, and you would have a strong argument. If I may misquote Dylan Thomas (and why not? Everyone else does): "Praise the Lord, we are a 'humourous' nation", and leave it at that.

If you have your ideas on Welsh Humour, don't write to me, send them to the learned symposium in Cardiff. All I ask of you is, that if you think what I say and do is funny to you, just laugh, and I promise not to ask you why.

P.S. Thank you Dai and Wil for everything.

Ryan Davies July, 1976

One afternoon in my office, my assistant, Mair Davies, who had worked on more of Ryan's television programmes than anyone else, told me that Ryan and his family were at Reception. We both went down to meet them and to have tea. As soon as Bethan and Arwyn saw me, they ran toward me and I swung them in the air as I had done since they were little children. They were going to America to visit Brian Jones, who had been their friend since their school days and their best man. Mike Evans was with them to drive them to Heathrow. Over tea, Ryan did not talk much about his much-deserved and much-needed rest – he talked about the Welsh Theatre Company's next production. He had been invited to take part in three of Molière's one-act plays, playing the lead in every one of them. He had not played Molière since our first play together in the Normal College in 1957. The discussion over tea had come to an end. Mair and I walked to the entrance of Broadcasting House. Both of us waved to them as they drove away. I was never to see my great, close friend again.

# *Losing Ryan*

THE TELEPHONE RANG in my home at about nine o'clock on 22 April, 1977. It was my friend Rhiannon:

"Have you heard?"

"What?"

"Ryan is dead."

There are no words, or arrangement of words, that I can put together to explain my feelings at that moment. All I could do was to clutch at a straw, hoping with every sinew in my body that someone had got the message wrong. I knew that Ryan's Mam was staying at his house while he was away so I phoned her. When I got through she verified the saddest news of my life. Ryan is dead. I phoned Mair at the office and she was very disturbed. When I arrived at Broadcasting House I was confronted by many people. I remember my friend Emyr Daniel, who works with our news department, telling me that everyone there was numb, wordless, very sad. They were people who dealt with the tragedies and mishaps of life on a daily basis, and – outwardly at least – they appear to find it difficult to express emotion. This morning, the newsroom was like a tomb – everyone reacted as if a member of their own family had passed away.

Since that day, so many people have told me what they were doing; where they were when they heard of Ryan's death. Everyone seemed to own a little part of him. Everyone had their own secret memory of him.

Gwenlyn, David and myself went down to Heathrow to meet Irene and the children when they returned from America the following day. Mike and the family doctor, Dr Brian Cronin, were already there, and I told Mike that we would not make ourselves conspicuous unless Irene wanted to see us. The flight was late and we waited a long time. Irene did want to see us, and I know that the years of friendship were of some help in alleviating the enormous emotional strain that she felt at that moment. Brian Jones had come all the way from Buffalo with Irene and the children, and he travelled to Cardiff with us in our car. We heard the story of Ryan's death from him and from Irene months later.

They had had a very relaxing holiday in Buffalo doing the normal tourist 'bit'. They visited the school attended by Brian Jones' children; Irene has a lovely tape-recording of Ryan talking to one of the American children. I think he was the teacher again. They visited Washington DC where they saw the many statues of past Presidents of the USA. When he saw the statue of Abraham Lincoln, Ryan became very quiet and meditative. He sat, looking at the statue for a long time as if, for that timeless moment, he had met a familiar soul. There are times, thank God, in all our lives when ordinary conjecture does not give us an answer. For a few seconds of our lives, perhaps, we are allowed the chance to understand eternity. Perhaps, in this moment by Abraham Lincoln's statue, Ryan was given his.

In Irene's own words, and in the report by Betty Hughes, we hear the sad story:

> "It was a relaxing visit and we took things very easily, apart from a few days in Washington DC seeing the sights. But there were vast changes in temperature – snow when we arrived, followed by intense heat and humidity – and this started up Ryan's asthma.
>
> The day before we were due to fly home, our friends were having a barbecue dinner in the garden. Ryan was helping with the preparations, and I suddenly realised just how bad his asthma had become. We decided to call a doctor but, by the time he arrived, Ryan had collapsed. He couldn't breathe and had to be given the kiss of life."
>
> The Welsh star was rushed by ambulance to the nearest hospital, which was about 15 minutes away, but he died of heart failure shortly afterwards.

Irene admits that she'd had a strange premonition about the holiday. "I had a strong feeling that something awful was going to happen," she said, "but I did not think it would be that. Even as I sat and waited at the hospital, I did not realise that Ryan was dangerously ill, despite the fact that a priest had been called. When they came to tell me he'd had a cardiac arrest and was on a machine, I still thought he would pull through. Then the doctors called me in and said he had suffered another two. When they added there was nothing more they could do, I felt completely numb.

She then had to face the ordeal of telling their two children. Bethan, who is now 13, went very quiet, but Arwyn, aged 10, rushed around the room. Then he said, "What about all the people back home?"

"I had three things that had belonged to Ryan – a pendant, a watch and a ring," Irene related with a catch in her soft voice. "I gave Bethan the pendant and Arwyn the watch. Since having that watch, he has grown up overnight. I kept the ring for myself."

Ryan was buried in the same cemetery as his father, Old Bethel, Glanaman, at the foot of the Black Mountain. I did not attend the funeral until everyone had left, but I came to the graveside before the earth had covered his coffin. I remember standing above his grave with David and Mary, Ronnie and Einir and Rhiannon, thinking of nothing but enormous fun, dance, song, merriment and that terrible mask of tears.

Since the funeral had been a family affair, many of us felt that something should be done in Ryan's memory. Geraint Stanley Jones and Jack wanted a memorial ceremony at his beloved theatre, the Grand in Swansea. I was asked to put it together in consultation with Irene, and David Richards directed the tribute which was transmitted live on radio.

I do not wish, even now, to express my thoughts. I prefer to record the words of other people:

**Alun Williams, Broadcaster:**

If we are to judge a man by the number and variety of his talents, the n he was without question the greatest of all Welsh entertainers.

We wonder what would have happened if, instead of slipping like quicksilver from one talent to the other, he decided to grab one of them and shake it by its throat. There would have been a lot of worried faces in whatever branch of the business he decided to develop. I, for one, was always grateful to him for steering clear of sporting commentary. If the question is going to be asked, can anyone fill his shoes? You know the answer as well as I. Never in Europe!

**The late Martin Williams, Past Administrator of the New Theatre, Cardiff, and Director of 'The Sunshine Boys':**

He was a most compassionate and understanding man. He loved people and he loved meeting people. He was always charming and never ruffled. At no time did I ever hear him speak a cross word to anyone, even under provocation.

**Gwyn Thomas, Playwright:**

The world of Welsh laughter stands at the moment roofless against the wind of this great loss. Wales has not been the easiest place in which to perfect comedy, to be a clown. We have been clouted by too may prophets and judges. We all tend to be touchy and awkward when anyone starts a bit of jesting at our expense. The average joke hides out in the hills and comes down only when the lights are out and the road is safe.

The miracle of Ryan was that he glided so gracefully and without disaster among the sensibilities of his own people. His gift of mime, the art of conveying sense, the rapture of gaiety or the sigh of sorrow without words was supreme. You remember the scene in the French film, 'The Children of the Gods', when Jean Louis Barrault perfects his technique of silent expression by walking constantly back and forth in front of the cabin in which sits a blind night-watchman. That is what Ryan reminded me of. His touch was as light as snow, as sure as fate. He had found his own brilliant, infallible way through the minefield of our dangerous emotions.

He would have projected the whole absorbing world of Welsh laughter and pathos without once awakening his Welsh audience into any resentful response. He understood and exultantly expressed the best that was in us. And if sometimes he spotted the worst it was shrugged away with a forgiving chuckle.

There was no kink or corner of the Welsh experience that did not fascinate him. He questioned me endlessly about what exactly had happened to me as a person born into a part of Wales where the Welsh language has been washed away by the English flood. He was puzzled by me. That is the great clown's first gift, the act of constant astonishment at the strangeness of other people. Nobody must be taken for granted or for nothing. We are all miracles.

When we first met he had heard me talking about the Spanish language. He had the idea that I was over here on loan from Patagonia to prop up the Eisteddfod Pavilion, then shaky. He was intrigued when I told him that my boyhood had been as full of Welsh chapel and eisteddfod as his own.

I told him of an eisteddfod at a village in the Vale of Glamorgan in which I had once competed as a boy soprano. The test piece was 'Y Fwyalchen' ('The Blackbird'). Four other lads from my part of the valley had all entered. We had agreed that whoever won we would share the prize. About sixpence. The IMF was not on the phone.

The eisteddfod was disturbed. A man who for ten years running had failed to qualify for the tenor solo for the over 55's had run berserk, tearing up the pegs of the big tent and molesting adjudicators. He had loosened the flap of canvas over the stage. One lad in a part-song event had strained himself singing alto in 'Ye Mariners of England' and holding up the flap like Victor Mature at Gaza. The adjudicator in our event was put off by the disturbances and in any case he did not like our song, 'The Blackbird'. Birds of this type played havoc annually with his beans or plums.

"Plums, I expect," said Ryan. "I knew a man from Llanfyllin who hated birds that dared to lay a beak on his fruit. A bit of veg, OK. But fruit – bang, bang."

The prize for the boy sopranos was withheld. My four companions and I made our way home very late. As we walked across the waun that divides the Vale from the Rhondda we sang 'Y Fwyalchen' right at the moon confident that we would at least get a hearing from that quarter.

"That's exactly how it should be", said Ryan. "The music should rise on easy, waiting wings from the laughter or the hurt, no matter which."

And he put his head back in that marvellous yearning gesture that he had and sang the Blackbird's song more beautifully than I will ever hear it sung again. Remembered flashes of his magic will keep filling our lives with affectionate light until they, too, have an end.

## Owen Edwards, Controller, BBC Wales:

It was here on this stage at the Grand in Swansea that Ryan was a king among his own people and particularly among the children. Over the last five years these walls have echoed to the joyous laughter of children flocking here in their thousands to be mesmerised by every sound and movement from this remarkable Pied Piper of Mirth. The Panto audience responded to him with an uninhibited warmth which he thrived on.

Ryan, like the true professional he was, worked unsparingly to build up a special relationship with every audience. He loved to have them close to him and he liked to do his own warm-up, whenever possible, before a show. I remember being particularly impressed by Ryan's intense professionalism during a recording in London of 'Fo a Fe'. There occurred half way through the recording one of those annoying but unavoidable technical breakdowns which meant holding everything for a few minutes. One would have understood if Ryan had gone backstage while everything was being sorted out but he went straight to that audience and kept them in fits of laughter so that when recording was resumed there had been no break in that vital relationship between him and his audience. For "this outstanding entertainer of his generation in Wales", as *The Times* rightly described him, did nothing by half measures. He sought perfection by being absolutely thorough, painstaking and immaculate and he expected the same from all who worked with and for him. The first-class, not the second-rate, was his yardstick and the giving of enjoyment to others meant the taking of infinite pains himself.

## *The Times*, 23 April, 1977:

Ryan Davies, whose appeal to Welsh audiences as an entertainer was heightened by his command of comedy in both Welsh and English, died suddenly yesterday while on holiday with his family in Buffalo, NY. He was 40 and was regarded in Wales as the outstanding entertainer of his generation.

He was more than a comedian – in fact, the product of the eisteddfod and the intimate evening's entertainment which could bring out talents as pianist, harpist, baritone, mimic, clown and author of his own material.

He also enhanced the scope of the Welsh language on television programmes and was always anxious to maintain a very high standard, avowing that if he put over rubbish his audience would switch at once to something better in English.

Born in Glanaman, Dyfed, he trained as a teacher at Bangor, and went on to the Central School of Speech and Drama. Back in Wales he paired with Ronnie Williams and later developed as a solo performer.

He leaves a wife and two children.

**Michael D. Evans, Ryan's friend, Personal Manager, and Secretary of Ryan's Memorial Fund:**

> Ryan's death came at a time when the future held so much for him. In his last 12 months, I saw him entertain over a quarter of a million people; that was his aim in life – to give as much pleasure to as many people as possible. This he achieved over and over again, but sadly at great personal cost.
>
> As a public figure, Ryan never attempted to cut himself off, but he always insisted that nothing should interfere with his family and the bringing up of his children, Bethan and Arwyn. To attempt this in the entertainment business is difficult. To achieve it – which he did – is rare.
>
> Many will treasure the friendship they held with Ryan and those who met him will not fail to remember his kindness and sincerity. Everyone will have their personal stories to tell of Ryan – they will all make you smile and that is exactly how he would want to be remembered.

At the time of writing, the Ryan Davies Memorial Fund will soon award its first scholarship. The Fund, set up soon after Ryan's death, aims to assist young Welsh talent in the Arts, particularly Music and Drama, and in so doing perpetuate the memory of Ryan.

The Fund currently stands at £25,000 and this sum has been realised by the encouragement and support of many organisations throughout Wales and England which Ryan assisted during his career. Many fundraising concerts have taken place, from the Wembley Conference Centre to chapels in Glanaman, involving many artists including Harry Secombe, Stuart Burrows, Frankie Vaughan, Massed Choirs and those who have worked closely with Ryan. The fundraising continues to give young people in Wales every opportunity to further their training.

As a personal tribute to their friend, Ryan, the staff of the Grand Theatre, Swansea, have erected a plaque in the foyer of the theatre in his

*Ryan.*

memory. It shows a portrait of Ryan, beautifully recreated by Harold Christie, and it stands as a permanent reminder of his contribution to the theatre.

A few months ago, my wife – by chance, her name is also Irene – and I were invited to Swansea by Ryan's Irene to see a production of Brecht's play 'The Caucasian Chalk Circle' performed by the West Glamorgan Youth Theatre. Arwyn had a minor part in the play. I was sitting next to Bethan when Arwyn made his entrance. It was an entrance I had seen many times before.

A few months before, I had taken Arwyn fishing to Newport, Pembrokeshire. We were fishing in the River Nevern. The tackle he was using had belonged to his father and his grandfather before him. Everything was arranged perfectly – the flies, the hooks, the gut; all arranged, clean and untangled in their own little compartments inside the little case. Arwyn hooked a fish and drew it to the bank, excited but disciplined as I had instructed him. I helped him to draw the hook out of the silver trout's mouth. He turned to me and said,

"Don't hurt him, Uncle Rhydd."

There are moments in everyone's life that are eternal.

# Also by Ryan

**CANEUON RYAN**
The original Ryan songbook
— 11 of his most popular
songs arranged for piano
and guitar.
0 86243 061 5
*£4.95*

**Y GÂN OLA'**
Ryan's "Last Song"
arranged by his son,
Arwyn.
0 86243 430 0
*£1.95*

**To appear in 2003:**
a completely new,
bilingual collection of
Ryan's unpublished
songs, arranged by
Arwyn (music) and
Bethan (words).

# Some other publications...

**THE DYLAN THOMAS TRAIL**
**David Thomas**
A guide to the West Wales villages and pubs where Dylan Thomas wrote and drank.
0 86243 609 5
£6.95

**SOSBAN FACH**
**ed. Stuart Brown**
Great collection of 30 rugby club songs for Saturday night!
0 86243 134 4
£4.95

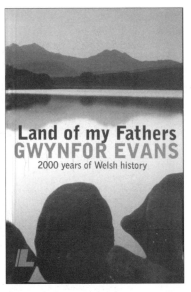

## THE LAND OF MY FATHERS
**Gwynfor Evans**
Lucid, masterful, comprehensive, passionate history of Wales – essential reading!
0 86243 265 0
*£12.95*

## ETERNAL WALES
**Gwynfor Evans & Marian Delyth**
Beautiful, coffee-table book with unforgettable images of Wales; text by Gwynfor.
0 86243 363 0
*£24.95*

## BLACK MOUNTAINS
### David Barnes
The recollections of a South Wales miner – an extraordinary tale of suffering and survival.
0 86243 612 5
£6.95

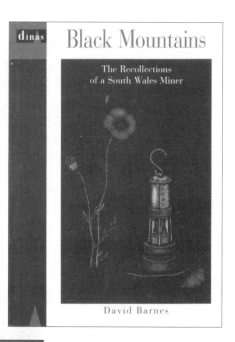

## THE WELSH LEARNER'S DICTIONARY
### Heini Gruffudd
At last, a really useful dictionary for Welsh learners, with 20,000 words and phrases.
0 86243 363 0
£6.95

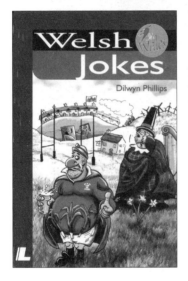

**WELSH JOKES,
WELSH TALK**
– just two of the
very popular titles
in our "It's Wales"
series. For full
details, see our
Catalogue or
website.

For a full list of
publications, ask for
your free copy of our
new Catalogue — or
simply surf into our
secure website,
**www.ylolfa.com**,
where you may order
on-line.

TALYBONT, CEREDIGION, CYMRU (WALES) SY24 5AP
*ffôn* (01970) 832 304
*ffacs* 832 782
ylolfa@ylolfa.com
www.ylolfa.com–